MARY CRAWFORD BROWN

Your ever loving
Mary C. Brown

IN 1915.

MARY CRAWFORD BROWN

A MEMOIR

JAMES STRAHAN, D.D.

*With three illustrations in colour and eight portraits
in photogravure*

JAMES CLARKE & CO., LIMITED
13 & 14 FLEET STREET, E.C.4
1920

Cahill & Co., Ltd., London, Dublin and Drogheda.

ERRATA.

Page 29, line 6, for "should" read "could."
,, 56, ,, 4 from foot, for "haux" read "hauts."
,, 69, ,, 6 from foot, omit "her."
,, 100, ,, 2 from foot, for "spirit" read "Spirit."
,, 142, ,, 17, for "had" read "has."
,, 155, ,, 4 from foot, add "s" to "exhibition."

CONTENTS

ILLUSTRATIONS and PORTRAITS

PREFACE

It has been the writer's privilege to escape for a little while from the routine of special studies and to hold communion in spirit with one whose passage through this world has been to many a convincing evidence of the Divine reality of our Christian faith. This book is written in order that every reader may enjoy the same vivid and sacred friendship, heart yet speaking to heart though the voice is still.

When a Scotsman, after but a short stay in Ireland, was invited to prepare the Memoir of a gifted and gracious Irishwoman—a beautiful soul if there has been one in our time—the difficulties were so great and obvious that he could only decline a task for which he seemed to have no fitness. This happened more than once, but there were influential people, in particular some beloved missionaries, whose mild persistence could not be ignored, and the decisive appeal was made by the sisters of one of the writer's first and dearest Irish friends, affectionately remembered by all his comrades as " Willie Wilson of Coleraine," whose cross-marked grave in France James Pyper of Duncairn and the writer visited together in the last month of the war.

If thoughts of foolhardiness and incompetence have sometimes haunted the biographer in the fulfilment of his promise, he has refused to heed them, being assured that tasks in hours of insight willed can be through hours of doubt—there have been none of gloom—fulfilled.

The aim has been to make the Memoir, as far as possible, a self-portraiture, that being the best way to secure perfect fidelity to life. Warm thanks are due to two of Mary's Parisian girl-friends and life-long correspondents, Mlle. Hélène Wehrlin, of Alsace, and Miss Ella Martin, of Newry, County Down, who had the wisdom to perceive the value of her letters, written to the one mostly, though not invariably, in French, and to the other nearly always in English. By preserving each a sheaf of her intimate, self-revealing messages, and putting them all at the writer's disposal, they have considerably eased his onerous task. It is hoped that the numerous extracts from her French letters will read smoothly enough in English. Some fragments of her correspondence were also forwarded by Mary's Norwegian school-friend, Emma Thomas, now Mrs. Ramm. And after the Memoir was almost completed, some fifty letters written to her son Oliver during his period of service in Mesopotamia and convalescence in India came into the writer's hands. These are in some ways the most valuable of all.

The other data which have been woven into the Memoir have been obtained in the course of talks with Mary's kinsfolk in Belfast and at Donaghmore,

with her comrades in Church and Zenana work, with
her missionary friends at home on furlough, with her
associates in musical and educational circles, and with
young people whose spirits were touched to finer
issues by fellowship with her. Some of her friends,
such as Dr. William Park and Dr. George Thompson,
Mrs. R. H. Boyd and Miss Helen Waddell, have given
their memories and impressions in letters as well as
in conversation. In the use of the materials submitted
to him the writer has, of course, had a perfectly free
hand, and he alone is responsible for the manner in
which everything has been presented.

The book is pre-eminently a missionary biography.
That the work of Foreign Missions is the supreme
task of the Church Catholic, and that none of us can
follow Christ at all without following Him in spirit to
the ends of the earth, are facts recognised in our day
more fully than they have ever been since the time of
the Apostles. In a new epoch, and what looks like a
new earth, Christ's allied armies are at last being
mobilised for the grand crusade of the world's evangelisation. Faith is the invincible power that conquers
the world, and aught short of this victory is " too
light a thing."

The writer is conscious that his own share
in the great task has been almost nil. After
volunteering as a student for the Indian Mission Field
and being offered a Missionary College professorship
at three-and-twenty, he was, like the subject of this
Memoir, medically forbidden to go. But no one who
has once heard the Christian soldier's " marching

orders " can ever forget them, and it would be good indeed if this imperfect Life of a brilliantly-gifted contemporary, who never saw a heathen land, but of whom it is certain that Foreign Missions " haunted her like a passion," were used to fan the fire of missionary enthusiasm among the ministers, students, and people of the Church.

" We missionary folk," writes one of themselves in *The International Review of Missions,* " stand convinced that Christianity, as taught to the children and as practised in the nation, has been robbed of force and motive power by the strangely general omission of its missionary bearing, its missionary ideals, and its missionary demands." It is with a deep sense of the justice of this reflection, and a humble desire to make some amends, that this Memoir is reverently inscribed to one company of those heroic men and women who above all others have unquestionable claims to stand in the true Apostolic Succession.

Thanks are due to Messrs. Chatto and Windus, Publishers, for permission to use R. L. Stevenson's verses, " Yet, O stricken heart," p. 189.

Mary Crawford Brown

CHAPTER I

THE LIGHTED TORCH

" SHE was the saint of our Church," were the quietly
emphatic words with which one of the Foreign
Mission conveners began a talk regarding the Christian lady whose memory this book seeks to enshrine.
" Yes," was the response, " and surely a very human
saint ! " The adjective may well be stressed. Ireland
was the Isle of Saints—men and women burning with
missionary zeal—at a time when the greater part of
Europe was still shrouded in heathen darkness, and
Ireland has saints, both Roman and Protestant, among
her daughters to-day. Not a few of the former, perfectly true to their own ideal, are to be found, praise
God, among the sisters who dedicate their lives to
acts of piety and charity. The latter are taken
captive by a larger, fairer, and, one cannot help
thinking, far more truly Christian ideal of the

spiritual life. Surrendering none of the personal liberty and moral dignity which Christ conferred on woman, and choosing, in general, the home as the best of all spheres of Christian activity, they not only cultivate the arts and graces which, as handmaids of religion, refine and beautify human life, but at the same time widen, ennoble, and hallow all their interests by a steadily burning enthusiasm for the Church's imperial task of carrying the Gospel of Divine love into every land. Alien in spirit to nothing in this wonderful life of ours, except the sin which has invaded it, and loving the whole great human family for which Christ died, they are passionately earnest in claiming the earth and its fulness for the Lord.

May the portrait of one of our modern Protestant saints, splendidly Catholic in the only true sense of the term, whom France gave to Ireland and Ireland to the world, prove how free and full, how richly and nobly human is the life which, under constraint of Christ's love, blends with the desire to adorn the doctrine of God our Saviour in all things, the high ambition to make His way known upon earth and His salvation among all nations.

Mary Crawford, the only daughter of Sir William and Lady Crawford, of Mount Randal, Belfast, was well-born in the highest sense of the word, for she received as a child what one of the Hebrew Prophets calls " the goodliest heritage of the nations."* Through her parents she fell heir to a noble, perhaps

*Jer. iii. 19. (R.V. margin).

a unique tradition of missionary zeal and service. Her paternal grandfather was one of the first four young Scotsmen, and her maternal grandfather one of the first two young Irishmen, who heard and obeyed the Divine call to go and begin the evangelisation of India's millions. When Alexander Crawford set out from Scotland for the East in 1822, and again when James M'Clure Glasgow left the shores of Ireland in 1840, their departure aroused an extraordinary interest among all who could discern the signs of the times. They were men compassed about with a great cloud of witnesses. As they sped forth with their comrades to carry their lighted torch into the darkness of heathendom, every earnest mind in their homelands was stirred, every tender heart moved by epoch-making events which seemed to betoken a return of apostolic fervour to the modern Protestant Church. Those two heroic pioneers became bosom friends, and before the younger of them ended his race, the missionary torch, burning very brightly, passed into the hand of a girl who, with the blood of both coursing in her veins, seemed to inherit a double portion of the spirit of her fathers.

The ancestors of the Crawfords were living a century ago in classic Tweedside. Mary's grandfather Alexander, the son of a Peebles working mason who met his death by some accident, received that education which Scotland knows how to bestow on every "lad o' pairts," and the University of Edinburgh opened her portals to him. Sacred learning was more precious in his eyes than secular. Bred in the

National Church in the early days of her Evangelical
Revival, and fired with the spirit of Brainerd and
Carey, he offered himself to the Scottish Missionary
Society (founded in 1796), and was sent to India a
year before Reginald Heber began his work in
Calcutta, and seven years before John Wilson landed
at Bombay.

With him went his young wife Anna Gardner, the
daughter of an Edinburgh man of business, whose
marriage was the happy end of a charming romance.
There never was any doubt of Anna's admiration for
the brave youth who had volunteered to go out into
the dark places of the earth. But the course of true
love did not run smooth in her home down in the old
Edinburgh Pleasance. Her parents were divided on
the great question of her future, for while the mother's
heart leapt up at the thought of giving a beloved
daughter to the Mission Field, the more cautious, yet
not less Christian father, doubting if " a man of fair
complexion " could stand the Indian climate, stoutly
refused his consent to the proposed union. So
Alexander Crawford had to set out sorrowfully
for India alone. But his ship was delayed for
three weeks in the Thames, and three weeks
afforded time enough for the young people to exchange
affectionate letters once more, time for the mother
and daughter to plead as they had never pled
before, time for the doubting father to change his
mind at last, and time, even in coaching days, for the
overjoyed lover to speed back to Edinburgh and perfect
his happiness.

REY ALEX CRAWFORD.

Mʀˢ CRAWFORD.

REY JAMES GLASGOW, D.D.

Mʀˢ GLASGOW.

Before the biographer lies the long and now much faded letter to Anna, dated December 30th, 1822, which induced her good father to relent. It is a document naturally treasured in the Crawford family. The style, though not the matter, somehow reminds one of Jane Austen. " It would," says the earnest suitor, " have afforded me unspeakable pleasure if, by one or other of those attempts which your dear mother made, the barriers had been removed, and we had been permitted to enter on the work of the Lord, and to assist each other and strengthen and consolidate our mutual affection while we swept over the face of the mighty deep. But I must, and I trust I do, say, ' The will of the Lord be done.'

" I cannot help wondering, however, at your worthy father. O, my dear, help me both by your prayers and your affectionate conduct to obtain from God this blessing for him and his family. The permission, the high command must come from God, and patiently to wait in the due use of means, cheerfully to submit to His will, and actively to discharge the filial duties so long as they are within your power, is the direct way to obtain the desire of your heart. May the Spirit who ' maketh intercession for the saints according to the will of God ' lead and guide you in this and everything else that will be for His glory.

" My dear Anna, it is perhaps not out of time yet. Perhaps you wonder at me now, and are saying, ' Whence can this hope arise? ' I long ago told you that I would not lay aside all hope till I had set my foot on deck. Now, my Anna, the Lord has lengthened

B

out the time once more.   The day after I received your
kind and affectionate letter, we called on the owner
of the *Euphrates,* and he told us she would not sail
for three weeks at the soonest, a space sufficiently
long to settle that important business, much longer in
fact than some have taken for acquaintance and all.
I received this day from a doctor such information
with regard to my constitution and health as goes to
do away completely with the feeling which rested in
your father's mind about fair complexion.   Also from
Mrs. R., who has been in India five years; her husband
is fair and has been in a state of excellent health all the
time—and many others whom she knows personally.
This does not insure my life, but it does remove the
idea of your father. . .

" How pleasing it is to God to make a full and free
surrender in the face of difficulties and dangers in the
faith that He will give strength and protection.   But
what need to dwell on these things, for I am perfectly
persuaded that you are self-devoted in this very spirit.
I heartily wish, not so much for my own sake
as for the interest of that glorious cause to
which I have devoted myself, that your dear
father and friends would in the same spirit
and the same mind devote you to the same service.
My heart is yours, my arms are open, the ship is
ready, the field of labour is empty, and the heathen
are perishing while the Son of God is promising
strength, giving the command, and affording every
possible encouragement to engage in the glorious
work.''

Human affairs are so mysteriously linked together that great effects seem often to depend on very trivial causes. Had the *Euphrates* obtained a fair wind and sailed out of the estuary of the Thames at her appointed time, many things would doubtless have been altogether different. There are chains of circumstance in every life which can never have been forged by chance. The wind bloweth where it listeth, but even the winds and the sea are obedient to a higher than natural law.

The Edinburgh girl of nineteen, who was so irresistibly wooed and so happily won for the Indian Mission Field, belonged to a Scottish family well known for its attachment to the evangelical and missionary cause. "Two ever-welcome visitors in her brother's house," writes her grand-nephew,* "were William Burns, afterwards the devoted missionary to China, and Robert Murray M'Cheyne. I have heard one of my aunts say that more than once she was awakened in the morning by hearing M'Cheyne's sweet tenor voice singing the morning Psalm with which he always began his private devotions. It was no more disturbing than the song of a thrush or blackbird in the summer morning. . . . It was a speech by M'Cheyne in the Synod of Ulster that led to the foundation of the Irish Presbyterian Mission to the Jews."

In that evangelical circle Anna had been one of the first to catch the true missionary spirit,

* Mr. Thomas Gardner, Manager of the Edinburgh Life Assurance Company.

and most gladly would she have spent all her life in the Indian Mission Field. But a second time the whole disposing of her lot was "of the Lord," who now seemed to thwart rather than further her purpose. Her cautious father's fears were after all partially justified. Seven years of earnest and fruitful labour at Bankot, seventy miles south of Bombay, were all that her husband was permitted to give to India. The state of his health obliged him to bring his family home, and to his great sorrow he was forbidden to return to the East. But what a sacred memory for himself and his children—the eldest ones Indian-born—were those seven missionary years! And the home-coming which involved a heavy loss to the Scottish Mission in India proved a great gain to Ireland, for after spending a short time in England as one of Lady Huntingdon's preachers, Mr. Crawford accepted a call to the First Presbyterian Church of Randalstown, in County Antrim. There he built for himself the home of "Maine Mount," which has been dear to three generations of Crawfords, and there he laboured for the rest of his life, doing very much all the time to foster a missionary spirit in the Church and land of his adoption. Old Randalstown people* still remember his saintly character, his fervent preaching, his frequent open-air services, and one of his converts has told the writer how his face used to shine like Stephen's whenever he spoke of the love of Christ.

* As the venerable Dr. West, of Antrim, testifies.

MAINE MOUNT, RANDALSTOWN.

MOUNT RANDAL, BELFAST.

The heroine of the above romance, who left Edinburgh ninety-eight years ago to serve Christ in the Indian Mission Field, was Mary Crawford's grandmother. In the Bankot Mission House and the Randalstown Manse she became the mother of five sons and five daughters, to whom she left the sacred heritage of her Christian faith and missionary zeal. Eight of them have ended their pilgrimage. The two youngest sons, Robert and William—now Sir William, Mary's father—are spending the peaceful eventide of life in their Belfast homes.

Grandmother Anna survived her husband by six-and-twenty years. " Keen and vigorous in mind, well versed in evangelical literature,"* she lived at Maine Mount till Mary was a girl of fifteen, and it is significant that they had many opportunities of talking together. The Rev. F. S. Gardiner of Kingstown, Mary's cousin, depicts a closing scene in the life of this aged saint, who must have greatly resembled the Anna of the Gospel story.

" I remember her well," he writes, " and her memory is very fragrant to me. The first time I visited Ireland with my father, and stayed at Maine Mount, I was too much of a boy to be taking much note of character. But in 1882, when I was ordained minister of First Coleraine, she sent for me, and I shall never forget that interview. Her eyes brightened when I came into her room, for she was eagerly expecting me. The spiritual atmosphere was very tense. She realised that she would soon pass within the veil, and

* As the Rev. J. E. Ferguson, of Randalstown, recalls.

she anticipated it with holy joy. I remember her telling me that she had been praying for me during the hour in which I was being ordained. And before I said good-bye, she placed her hands on my head and offered up a tender prayer that mine might be a soul-saving ministry. I left the room feeling that I had been in the presence of a saint of God, very ripe for her heavenly home. In a few days she had gone to be with Him whom her soul loved."

Mary became heir to an equally noble missionary tradition through her mother, now Lady Crawford, whose father, Dr. James M'Clure Glasgow, was one of the most notable Ulstermen of his time. Sprung, as his name indicated, from some old Scottish stock, and born at Clough in County Antrim, he became a Belfast student of rare distinction, excelling first as a mathematician and then as a Hebraist. He was ordained to the ministry at Castledawson, in County Derry, but he had laboured there only a short time when he received an unmistakable call to a higher and harder service, being selected by the first General Assembly of the united Presbyterian Church in Ireland as one of its two first missionaries to India.

Mr. Glasgow regarded the mandate of his brethren as indicating for him the will of God. Soon after his appointment he married Mary Wightman of Lisburn, and together they sailed for the East amid the prayers of the whole Church. Acting on the advice of John Wilson, the apostle of Western India, the Irish Mission Board chose the province of Kathiawar as its first field of operations, and there Mr. Glasgow gave his Church " four-and-twenty years of exceptionally toilsome, trying and telling service."* He became a Fellow of the University of Bombay, and a member of the Royal Asiatic Society. Coming home in 1864, he was appointed by the General Assembly as Professor of Oriental Languages, and became widely known as the author of a learned commentary on the Apocalypse. †

He is best remembered, however, as a man of missionary enthusiasm, who longed for the conversion of Jew and Gentile, putting his deepest emotions into such wistful verses as these :

> Oh ! when shall those who slumber
>   As still and deep as death,
> A vast uncounted number,
>   Feel the awaking breath?

> When shall the Jews who stumble,
>   And their Messiah spurn,
> In heart and spirit humble
>   Back unto Him return?

Dr. Glasgow lived till 1890, the fiftieth year of the Church's Indian Mission, and it was a striking fact that the old pioneer went to his rest on the very day before the public celebration of the historic event, as if he had received a call to keep his Jubilee in Heaven rather than on earth.

* Robert Jeffrey, *Indian Mission of the Irish Presbyterian Church*, p. 171.

† Published by T. & T. Clark in 1872.

Five daughters had been born to Mr. and Mrs. Glasgow in India. The two eldest died there in infancy, and the others, Mary, Annie, and Harriet, were brought home, as all Anglo-Indian children must be, for their upbringing. They were educated at Walthamstow School for the Daughters of Missionaries—since removed to Sevenoaks—and always looked back upon those years with grateful memories, the school being one of high ideals and warm interest in missionary enterprise. Annie Coulson Glasgow, who was born at Surat, one of the chief cities of Gujarat, was but eighteen when she became the wife of the youngest son of the Randalstown Manse. The two pioneer missionary families, representatives of the purest evangelical faith of Southern Scotland and Northern Ireland, were thus happily united. And doubtless they praised God in their hearts.

William and Annie Crawford spent the first two-and-twenty years of their wedded life in France. At an early age he had given clear indications of possessing an unusual aptitude for business. Entering the service of the York Street Flax Spinning Company, Belfast, in his seventeenth year, he was doing a man's full work before he was eighteen. In 1862 he was sent to represent the firm in Paris, where the business prospered under his care, in spite of great difficulties he had to face, and his imperfect knowledge, at that time, of the language.* After four years he came home to marry, and he and his young wife began their

* His youngest son Harry is now at the head of the business in the French capital.

wedded life in a flat of the Rue Montholon. Their first child was born on January 14th, 1867, and named Mary, after her grandmother, Mary Wightman. In the end of 1887, when Mr. Crawford was appointed Managing Director of the Company, the family came to live permanently in Ireland, and three years ago, amid the turmoil of the great war, the golden Jubilee was quietly celebrated at Mount Randal, so named by its owner in remembrance of his happy childhood at Maine Mount in Randalstown.

That this captain of industry has all along been in warm sympathy with missionary enterprise might be proved in many ways. It is enough to record a recent utterance of his. "You may take it from me," he said, "that my last and greatest and dearest wish is that the Gospel may be preached throughout the whole world."

This ardent desire, this selfless missionary passion, has been Ireland's "divine fire," which has won for her a richer than any earthly glory. It lighted a thousand torches in that golden age of Irish Christianity, when Ireland was known in Christendom not only as the Island of Saints—by itself a poor enough designation—but as the School or Hive of Missions, in which an unnumbered host of teachers and preachers were trained and consecrated for Christ's service in the heathen lands of the world.

"Oh passion of holy love !
Oh sacrificial people ! "

And just because Christianity is true, and no Christian

nation **ever** permanently forgets its past, the great heart of Ireland will yet again melt and glow in sympathy with Him who said :

> I AM COME TO SEND FIRE UPON THE EARTH,
> AND WOULD IT WERE ALREADY KINDLED !

CHAPTER II

THE DEW OF YOUTH

MANY of Mary's friends seem to have imagined that she was Parisian by birth, an error which crept into the Memorial Number of *Woman's Work* (January, 1919). Three of her five brothers began life in Paris, but Mary was born in Claremont Street, Belfast, and carried to her Paris home in nurse's arms when six weeks old. She was the only daughter in a family of six, the youngest of whom died in his second year. Before the departure from the city of her birth, she was baptised by Dr. James Morgan, minister of Fisherwick Church, in the old place of worship which stood on the site now occupied by the Assembly Hall and Church House. Her reception as a babe into the fellowship of the Church by so earnest and ardent a friend of Missions added yet another link to the mystic chain which was to bind her—to " thirl " (thrall) her, as her Scots forbears would have said—for all her life to Christ's cause in the Mission Field. Having been the leading spirit in the inauguration of the Church's

Foreign Mission, Dr. Morgan was naturally chosen as the first Convener of the Mission Committee, an office which he held for over thirty years, in the last two or three of which he had Dr. William Fleming Stevenson as his coadjutor.

Mary's journey from Ireland to France in unconscious infancy foreshadowed many comings and goings on her part between the two countries. During her Parisian childhood and youth she visited Ireland, with her parents and brothers, about a dozen times, always in summer, and generally for a couple of months at a time. Her longest sojourn, lasting over a year, was occasioned by the Franco-German war. In the summer of 1870, just before the outbreak of hostilities, she and her brother Alek, who was barely two years old, were hurried away across the Channel, and the family did not return to France until the disastrous campaign, the siege of Paris, and the terrors of the Commune were all past. Mary had begun life three years and a half before the fall of the Second Empire, and she was to spend over seventeen years in Republican France.

The little tales which form the record of her early years suggest to the imagination as bright and thoughtful a child as any fond parents could wish to call their own. She first opened her eyes on all the wonder and beauty of the world in her daily rambles through the *Jardin des Tuileries,* near which was her home before the war. This famous Garden, where the Royal Palace stood till the Communists burned it down in 1871, has long been the favourite promenade of grown-up Paris, and the special paradise of nurse-maids and children. On the north side it is skirted by the Rue de Rivoli, where Mary, when scarcely three, used to stop and recognise letters over shops, pointing and saying, " Ah, voilà A ! voilà B ! " and so forth. Little children should not know what dark storm-clouds were then gathering in the air. Mary's fourth year was the last in which Parisian boys and girls, seeing a splendid carriage flash past them in the pleasure garden, would ever exclaim, " Voilà l'Impératrice ! " When Eugénie, after many years, re-visited those once familiar scenes, she felt she had lost her identity. " It is another woman," she murmured, " who is looking out on the Rue de Rivoli."

One of Mary's cousins, Susan Horner, whose mother was the eldest of the Maine Mount family of ten, was often her playmate during the early visits to Ireland, and in later life Mary used to speak of Susan, who was seven years her senior, as "ma grande amie d'enfance." Writing from Western America, where the greater part of her life has been spent, Susan revives some sunny memories of childhood.

" When I first knew Mary she was the happiest, merriest little child I ever saw, always ready to enter with the greatest zeal into any games or ploys that were prepared for her. I remember only one incident that wasn't *quite* right, and that happened one day in a row-boat, when she insisted on putting her little hat out into the water to swim, and there was no little difficulty in rescuing it.

" Though she was from the first a thoughtful and

serious child, she enjoyed playing innocent tricks on people. One day her brother Alek got a small bottle of perfume, of which he was very proud. He went strutting around sniffing it, and made quite a fuss over it, much to Mary's amusement. So getting hold of it next day, she carefully poured its contents into another bottle, and filled it up with water. When Alek took it up again, he found that it had lost its charm, so he consulted Mary about it, and she looked very grave and sympathetic. Just then he remembered that he had a cold in his head, and therefore concluded that he must have lost his sense of smell ! ''

Quite early she began to have day dreams. '' When she was about seven or eight,'' Susan says, ''she either read, or heard read, one of Hesba Stretton's stories about the slums of London. It made a great impression on her, and afterwards, when we sat alone, or went for walks together, she took the greatest delight in talking over and over the lovely things she would do for the poor people if she were rich. Some of her little projects were certainly beautiful if impracticable.''

From her childhood she had the artistic fancy which creates similes and parables. '' One Sunday morning, when she was about eight, she said to her mother, ' Mama, I was thinking last night when you were passing through my room so often, putting out our clothes for this morning, and the lamp kept coming and going, that the light was like joy and the darkness like sorrow, and you know there is more sorrow than joy in this world. Then after you had got all done, you said Good Night and shut the door. That was like death. But this morning, when I woke up, the sun was shining, and the birds were singing, and I heard the fountains playing. That was Heaven.' "

She began quite early, too, to give a reason for the hope that was in her. " One day," writes Susan, " she was sitting in the room where some grown folks were talking, and in the conversation a gentleman with a sceptical turn of mind expressed his opinion that it was very unlikely that God—if there was a God— would listen to or answer the prayers of individuals. Then a child's sweet voice broke in—' I *know* that God answers prayers, because He has answered mine. ' "

Mary was about ten when her heart was first drawn to a Paris schoolmate of her own age, who was destined to be her confidential friend during all the next forty years. This was Hélène Wehrlin, the daughter of an Alsatian gentleman engaged in commerce at Mulhouse. Her mother still lives with her in Paris, 93 years of age, a charming old lady and a great reader. As a friendship so sweet, sacred and romantic sprang up between the Irish and the French girl (French to the core though her Alsace was then captive to Germany), and came to be so helpful to them both, it is well to hear how it began. " It was on a lovely afternoon in October, 1877," writes Hélène, " a few days after I entered Mlle. Viénot's school, that at the recreation hour I saw a lady arrive with three children, a little girl and two boys. I little thought that, despite the difference of nationality, there was about to begin between the new comers and me a friendship so firm that it has lasted through all the events of life. For four years the little girl, who became my dear friend Mary, and I continued to attend the same school, and thus we were daily together, our friendship becoming ever closer as time passed."

Through the eyes of this Alsatian friend we get glimpses of a thoughtful little girl, with fair hair and grey-blue eyes, attending the *Pension* of Mlle. Viénot, " always a good and punctual pupil, entering into all her lessons with zest; " playing with her brothers in the nursery at shipwreck on a desert island, in a boat of their own construction; listening with rapture to the singing of her canary birds; beguiling the tedium of chicken-pox by modelling a farmyard, a Venetian gondola, a steamboat, and an Italian house; spending her *sous* on flowering seeds in the Avenue des Ternes, and waiting their opening " with an interest as intense as that of the hero of Picciola watching the growth of his flower between the paving stones of his prison yard "; and talking of Ireland as a far-off land of dreams, in which the Giant's Causeway, Dunluce Castle, Newcastle and Slieve Donard were bathed in the magic of romance.

Mlle. Viénot, whose brother was a member of the Chamber of Deputies, was an exceptionally good teacher, and her influence was thoroughly Christian without being at all narrowing. Mary remained her pupil till she was about fifteen, and became an omnivorous reader of French and English books. She

MARY CRAWFORD, AGED 13.

learned the lessons of history, sacred and secular; she loved the wonderland of poets, Shakespeare, Tennyson and Burns being special favourites; and she browsed to her heart's content on the novels of Dickens, Thackeray and Sir Walter Scott. Among French books that charmed her were Jules Verne's fantastic stories and Alexandre Dumas' *La Tulipe Noire.* For more serious reading she had attractive books by such Protestant writers as Mme. de Pressensé and Mme. Bersier.

Her summer holidays were spent on the coast of Normandy or Ireland. Her first extant letter, written in French to Hélène from Carnlough, in County Antrim, when she was twelve, gives promise of the artistic sense and literary skill which she afterwards possessed in a high degree. "It is very lovely here," she tells her friend. "We have the sea just in front, and away to the right there is a fine promontory, of which I am going to attempt a sketch, and perhaps I shall send it to you in my next letter. The other day we went out boating in the evening, and saw the sun go down. It was extremely beautiful. The sea had a colour part of rose and part of lilac, and there was a belt of clouds in the sky which was at first all golden, and then became red, and in the end quite grey. . . . One would think that I must have time enough for writing here, but the day passes so quickly that evening comes before I know it."

Writing in July of the following year (1880) from Newcastle, County Down, Mary sends Hélène a drawing of the house in which she is staying; thanks her

C

warmly for the gift of a canary, which has arrived in safety from France and is now singing at the window; and announces that on the following Monday she is going to join a picnic party who are to spend the whole day " on a mountain called Slieve Donard, one of the peaks of the Mourne Mountains "—little dreaming how memorable the day and the mountain were to become to her in after years.

Next year we find her at Beuzeval in Normandy, a quiet old-world place where her family spent a good many summers, one of its chief attractions being a nice little Protestant Church in which it was a joy for old and young to worship. " I find it so agreeable," Mary writes to Hélène at the beginning of her stay there, " to do just what I please, without having to preoccupy myself with lessons, though I am not too lazy for that. Every morning, before breakfast, I teach Willy his German or geography, and after lunch we study the violin. I have also learned the dates of all the kings and queens of England down to Elizabeth; I am now going to learn those of France! You should also see all the serious books I have brought with me, and only three story books. We have already been bathing; yesterday it was so warm we could not do otherwise when we saw *tout le monde* in the water."

Two months later she is still at Beuzeval, and the holiday mood has somewhat subdued the love of work. She has read only a couple of books, whether of the improving or diverting class does not appear. She goes twice a week to the back room of a book-shop to study the piano, not having one in the house, and she still gives half an hour daily to the violin with Willy. But other things now fill up her days. She has bathed nineteen times, there are long walks on the shore, picnics when the weather is fine, and some fishing. She vividly describes a storm which burst upon her and her two eldest brothers one Sunday evening as they returned from Church. " All of a sudden we could neither see nor hear one another. The wind had risen and brought whirling clouds of dust. Everybody escaped home as fast as possible, without saying ' Good evening ' or anything else. When we got inside the storm was very great, but next day was as warm as if nothing had happened."

Two years later, when Mary was sixteen, she was again at Newcastle, and now she was deriving her greatest pleasure from art. " Are you drawing? " she asks Hélène in a letter. " You must do so, and then you will be able to show me the places where you have been on our return to Paris. Aunt Harriet and I have made many sketches and pictures, and though mine aren't very splendid I shall let you see them. The mountains here are at present magnificent, all covered as they are with heather in bloom. They make me despair, for I can never find the exact colour, but it is the rocks most of all that seem to be impossible to paint. The trees are much more easy, which is fortunate, for there are many of them." Another joy, she hears, awaits her up at Randalstown. " My uncle, with whom we shall be staying, has promised to let me ride on horseback, which I enjoy immensely."

Aunt Harriet (afterwards Mrs. John Acheson of Porta-
down) was the youngest of the three daughters whom
Dr. Glasgow had brought home from India. She was a
charming companion for Mary and the elder brothers,
and they all owed much to her goodness. When they
were small she taught them many things, including
Sunday games called " Bible Clocks " and " Sunday
Albums," and when Mary was old enough Harriet
and she spent many happy days sketching and botani-
sing together. Ere long, moreover, Harriet was able
to stimulate Mary's mind in yet another way, for she
inherited her father's literary gifts, and became well
known as a graceful and vigorous writer of both prose
and poetry. Some of the finest articles and poems in
Woman's Work were from her pen, and her Irish
ballads enjoyed much popularity.

Like every happy schoolgirl, Mary was always at
least as fond of play as of work. Having learned
lawn tennis in Ireland, she was keen to continue it in
Paris, and finding no court for the purpose—the game
was then almost unknown in France—she ingeniously
marked one off in the Bois de Boulogne with tape and
hair-pins, playing in that way with her brothers till a
proper court was prepared for them. She was an
excellent skater, loving the poetry of motion and
never losing a chance of indulging in the health-giving
exercise. She also danced well, and her brothers Alek
and James accompanied her now and then to dances.

Her real passion, however, was for piano music,
which was destined to fill a very large place in her life.
After beginning with a good lady teacher, she was fortu-

nate in obtaining a supremely gifted master, M. Victor
Moret, who came to the house to give her lessons.
Frequently he accompanied her on the violin, becoming
very enthusiastic as he warmed to the theme with so
responsive a pupil. Sometimes he brought his son
Ernest, a violin prodigy with a great shock of hair, to
play with her. In real music the master, wearied with
the daily round and common task, found refreshment
of spirit. Mrs. Crawford once remarked to him,
" You must get tired of hearing the same pieces
played by the same pupils." " Yes," he replied, " and
the same faults committed by the same persons ! "
He had some English pupils of whose performances
the best he could say was, " They have the notes."
British superficiality in matters artistic vexed his
righteous soul.

In Mary he had a student of a different order, in
whom he recognised a true musician—" the pupil
dreamed of (*l'élève rêvée*) by a professor," as
Hélène says—and he took the utmost pains in training
her. His method was unusual, and she acquired a
remarkable facility of execution at the expenditure of
much less energy and time than most pupils give to
the piano. His secret was simple enough. He
insisted on entire concentration of mind during the
time of practice, which he limited to an hour a day.
It is possible to play the scales while one is thinking
of anything under the sun, but against all wandering
fancies M. Moret set his face like a flint. Everything,
he repeated again and again, must be done with
thought, each note produced consciously and deliber-

ately. After an hour of such practice the mind would be utterly tired, but M. Moret knew the way to success and was remorseless. He would keep Mary playing the same scales, the same bars of music, in that absorbed manner day after day for weeks. Then he would say to her, " Now, play that quickly ! " The result was that however rapid her execution became, she gave every note its full value, and one felt that she was playing not only with her fingers but with her whole body and mind.

She became a pianist not alone because she had music in her soul and finely-strung nerves in her body. She succeeded by force of character. She had an instinctive feeling that things were going wrong whenever she found that, instead of being nervous, she was getting too cool and *insouciante*. On her eighteenth birthday we find her writing to Ella Martin, a Newry gentleman's daughter studying in Rouen, whose then recent Christmas visit to Paris proved the beginning of a warm and lasting friendship. After drawing a swallow flying low over water lilies, Mary says : " You know I told you I could not make myself feel nervous about my piece for Saturday. Well, even on Saturday I was so dreadfully indifferent and unconcerned that it required the greatest strength of will and the constant repetition of my favourite sentence, ' It's absolutely necessary,' to make me practise at all. However, I helped out the practising with a good deal of gymnastic exercises (so much that I really began to be afraid at the end that my arms would be so sore as to *prevent* my playing well instead of *help-*

ing it), and the piece went to the satisfaction of M. Moret, which was all I wanted. Since then I have had the luxury of not practising at all and being without any weight on my mind. I am devoting myself now mostly to painting. In Algebra I am at the binomial theorem; I haven't you to explain it, so I don't know if I shall make it out."

Her own strong will was reinforced by her father's. It was his invariable custom to hear her play in the evening after dinner, not only because he loved music, but because he knew it was good for her to have constant practice. Often the two would be all alone for hours in the drawing-room. He kept a complete list of the works she studied—the masterpieces of the best composers—and took them in regular succession, marking off each when she played it, so that she went through her repertoire time after time in the most systematic manner. It was no wonder if she used to say that her father did as much as M. Moret himself to make her a musician!

It has already been noted that Mary was also fond of sketching and painting, and at least one expert thought that she would have become a real artist if she had persevered. Among her Paris schoolfellows was a gifted Norwegian girl, Emma Thomas, who became another of her lifelong friends. Emma's artist sister married a brilliant young Norseman, M. Peter Nicolai Arbo, who was one day to be eminent as a court painter. Emma and Mary were the young " maids of honour " at the wedding. When Mary was a girl of fifteen she spent a summer at Sèvres, while the Arbos were living near by at Meudon. Mary received lessons from Mme. Arbo in oil colours, and found delight in painting china. M. Peter recognised her talent, and said to her one day, "What would you think of becoming a painter?" "It would be difficult," she answered. "All beautiful things are difficult," he rejoined, unconsciously echoing old Solon's proverb, χαλεπὰ τὰ καλά. Mary found life too short for excellence in more than one art, but some pictures on the walls of Mount Randal—particularly a splendid study of hollyhocks—indicate what she might have done if she had taken the Norse artist's suggestion to heart.

As Mary and all her brothers knew French at least as well as English, there was no need to worship in an English-speaking Church, though an occasional visit might be paid to the American Union Church in the Rue de Berri. For over a quarter of a century their father was a leading member of the French Reformed Church of Passy, near the Bois de Boulogne. He earned the distinction, conferred apparently for the first time on a foreigner, of being elected a member of the Conseil Presbytéral, which gave him the privilege of being a representative at the meetings of the Consistory of the Reformed Church of Paris. The minister of Passy Church, M. Abric, was a conscientious pastor of the old school, not a brilliant preacher, but a good man and a true friend, while his wife was a very clever Frenchwoman and a gifted writer. Mary and her brothers attended Passy Sunday

School for years, and it was M. Abric who in due time prepared her for her first Communion. Her mother used to accompany her when she went to receive the necessary instruction, as it is unusual for a girl to go out alone in Paris. While the teaching was being imparted, the mother would sit a silent listener, thinking her own thoughts. M. Abric prescribed themes for little essays, which Mary wrote with great care, and he thought she showed great understanding and spiritual insight. She, on her part, always spoke with gratitude of his wise counsels at that memorable time.

It need scarcely be said that Mary's mind and heart had been prepared in a good many other ways for the fellowship of the Christian Church. Though she was never given to wandering from her own fold, she did not miss the opportunity of hearing famous preachers. There was Pastor Eugène Bersier, who drew crowds, especially of fashionable ladies, to the big Etoile Church in the Avenue de la Grande Armée. He was an orator of the first order, whose books were translated into many European languages, and even if his sermons were rather too intellectual to grip young minds, it was always an education to listen to him. One could never forget the tone in which he would say at the close of a service, " Do not forget the poor " (*N'oubliez pas les pauvres*). Then there was Père Hyacinthe, whose *Conférences* drew " all the world " of Paris. Lady Crawford remembers going to hear him on a Good Friday afternoon, listening spellbound to an address lasting an hour and three-quarters, and coming away with the feeling that the whole service had not been more than half an hour. There was also the profoundly spiritual Theodore Monod, who still lives in retirement at Vincennes, near Paris, a greatly honoured and beloved octogenarian. He baptised Mary's third brother, William Monod Crawford. He will be remembered long as the author of a heart-searching hymn of experience, written not in French but in English, ending with the words:

> Higher than the highest heaven,
> Deeper than the deepest sea,
> Lord, Thy love at length hath conquered;
> Grant me now my supplication,
> None of self and all of Thee!

To mention one other name, Mr. D. L. Moody visited Paris in the course of his second European campaign (1881-4), and addressed a great meeting at the American Union Church. The whole Crawford family was there, and when the Evangelist, in his usual manner, invited all who intended to be out-and-out Christians to stand up and say "I will," Mary and her brothers were among those who responded. That was six-and-thirty years ago, but it is as vividly remembered as if it were an occurrence of yesterday.

Greater than all other factors in the development of Mary's character was the spirit of a home in which gaiety happily blended with gravity. Dullness was unknown where there was such an abundance and variety of young life. A faithful Parisian *bonne*, Claudine by name, who nursed the children one after the other, and remained in the family for nearly twenty years, provided daily entertainment with her witty

patter.   And Aunt Olivia (afterwards Mrs. Henry
Brown), who was Mrs. Crawford's companion for a
number of years, helped the children alike in work
and play, while she charmed everybody by the win-
someness of her disposition and the sweetness of her
voice. After so many years she is still remembered
as gliding about the house at her tasks while she sang,

> " O, happy day, that fixed my choice
>
> On Thee my Saviour and my God."

One of the old Prophets speaks of Hebrew house-
holds that had to form themselves into distinct groups,
and stand " every family apart."* Such cases occur
still.   " One thing," says Mary's eldest brother,
" which had a great effect upon us as a family was a
feeling of separateness. Living in a strange land, we
were thrown back very much upon ourselves, especially in such matters as Sabbath observance. Many
other English people in Paris did not adhere to the
old view as our parents did. And just because we
did not go with the stream, we felt that we were
largely separate, while it made us all the more united
among ourselves. Our father's strong convictions
had no less power over us than our mother's gentle
influence. To this day I remember his quiet talks
with us during our long walks through the streets of
Paris on the way to Church. ' It seems to me,' he
said one Sunday morning, ' that even if the blessings
of Christianity were only for this life, they are so over-
whelming that it would be worth while to be an out-

* Zech. xii. 12.

and-out Christian.' It was at such times that we really came to know him. His deep feelings were controlled by a calm judgment, and he generally had himself far too well in hand to betray any emotion, but there were times when it mastered him. When I went out to the Chinese Mission Field for the first time, he accompanied me as far as New York, and our parting there was a thing which I can never forget."

If such a father ever needed to speak a word of reproof to his daughter, he would do it in a way of his own. With a merry twinkle in moist eyes he said one day to the present writer, "Would you like to hear of the one little naughtiness which I can remember in Mary? When she was a girl of ten or eleven, she and I sat down one day to lunch alone in our Paris flat. In general she was well content with whatever food was set before us to eat, but there was something on the table that day which she did not like, and she grumbled a little. Surprised at what was so unlike her, I said it was very good food, but still she would not have it. So after a little I rose and said, 'Very well, Mary, you and I will not take any lunch to-day; we will just go into the next room.' And without another word we rose together from the table, leaving everything untouched." In the clash of wills, slight and yet so significant, his was the stronger. Very quietly, without any friction or waste of words, and with a little cheerful self-denial, he got his way. She yielded always to his gentle inflexibility, knowing that he was right. At the same time she imbibed his spirit and learned his secret. She was ever, it was said, "her father's own daughter."

One other most important element in Mary's spiritual growth remains to be mentioned. Her sixteenth year, she always said, was critical for her inner life. In the spring of 1882 she developed a serious lung trouble, which gave her parents grave anxiety, and for the first time she faced the solemnities of life and death. The family physician, Dr. Louis Monod, a cousin of Theodore, prescribed plenty of fresh air for her, and her father secured the summer lease of a house in the valley between Sèvres and Ville d'Avray. Before she left her Paris home she was so weak that she wrote to Hélène, "If I were to take a little turn in the Avenue for ten minutes or a quarter of an hour, I should be as tired on returning as if I had walked the whole day." But just when she felt so fragile in body, she yielded her whole soul as never before to the life-giving power of the Spirit of God. In a beautiful country garden, under the shadow of great trees, she had those "long, quiet times" (her own phrase) for thinking, reading and praying, which mark an epoch in the history of any soul. Others, too, were aiding the invalid in the best way possible. "At that time," says her father, "we prayed that she might be spared to us, and we dedicated her more fully than ever to God. He heard our prayer, and she lived to serve Him for other six-and-thirty years."

It is a great hour when one begins to know at first hand the majestic truths of religion, which are henceforth matters of immediate vision and personal experi-

ence, realised as facts on which one can live and die.
From this time onward there is a new seriousness and
spiritual depth in Mary's letters. She was nineteen
when she wrote thus to her Newry friend : " I have
found that the more I read the Bible, the more I love
it, and the more I feel the need of reading it. The
time when I first really came to love it was four years
ago. I was not at all strong for nearly two years.
At that time I chafed a good deal at being ill, but now I
see how God indeed best knows what is good for us.
If I had been quite strong I would not have had time
to think of these things." And again, two years
later, she says : " This evening Papa in reading at
worship came on some verses which I remember marking in my Bible six years ago, that ' blessed year.' I
was ill and had so much time for reading, and the
Bible was like a new book to me. For the first time
I was reading with open eyes, and Isaiah was the first
book I so read."

The net gains of such an experience cannot be
tabulated, but one benefit may be expressed in her
own way. " There is a knowledge which is deeper
than thoughts or words, and God is giving it to me.
This is a thing which has often come to me of late—
that to *know* God, to *love* God, to *serve* God, and
eternal life, are all the same thing. I remember being
told this as a child, and thinking I knew it. I find
now that I am just beginning to understand it."

As Mary recovered from her illness, she returned
with zest to her old occupations and recreations, adding some new ones to both. In July 1885 she went to

spend her holidays in Castle Mona, Port Erin, in the Isle of Man. There she played tennis, as she writes to her friend Hélène, on the very evening of her arrival from Paris, " in order to make up for not having slept all the previous night! And I assure you I received many compliments. Indeed I didn't play at all badly considering that I have not played for two years. You see, I don't need anyone to blow my trumpet, *tu comprends*? . . . I do not care for Douglas, which is a big town filled with tourists, but Port Erin is charming."

A letter from Paris in the following winter, when she was eighteen, throws a very cheerful light on her life at that time. " We had," she writes, " about a fortnight of frost in the end of January, and I had three jolly days skating. On Friday Hélène Wehrlin and I went together. On Monday Papa came with me, and I enjoyed myself immensely, meeting a good many people I knew. Then on Tuesday I went to Meudon, and had a good skate with Emma and her brother Edwin. But that night it thawed, so that was the end of it. . . . This evening M. Moret comes, and I think he will bring a piece for Emma and me to play on two pianos, for he is preparing for another recital. It is to be in about three weeks, and M. Moret has given me two horribly difficult new pieces to learn. I shall never know them, and am trying to resign myself to a total failure. One is a Ballade by Chopin, and the other a sonata of Beethoven to play with Ernest. I am most terrified of the sonata, as it is one of the most difficult and I know Ernest plays very quick.

. . . I am glad to say that a small ray of light is beginning to dawn on the binomials. Emma told Edwin that I was learning Algebra, and he was quite astonished, and I felt, and I am sure I looked, very proud. In this country girls don't learn anything of that sort."

Having become fond of riding, and finding it did her much good, Mary took some lessons at a Paris riding-school. One day her horse stumbled and threw her, but she contrived to slip down and alight on her feet. Her mother was present looking on, and the astonished riding-master, with a glance first at the one and then at the other, exclaimed, " She hasn't changed colour—nor her mother either ! " Probably he regarded them as good specimens of phlegmatic English ladies. After this Mary rode pretty frequently with her father in the Bois de Boulogne.

After her first Communion in Passy Church, it was natural that she began to teach in the Sunday School. She thereby entered upon a lifelong occupation to which she was to devote a great amount of earnest thought, while it gave her in return a deep and sacred joy. It was like her, too, that she soon began to induce her friends to share the work and the happiness. " One day," writes Hélène Wehrlin, " Mary eagerly persuaded me to come with her on the following Sunday morning to Passy Church in order to take charge of the younger children of her class, which had become very large. I yielded to her entreaties, and continued to teach a class there for twenty years."

By this time Mary was sometimes called to fill the

arduous *rôle* of domestic economist. Her grandmother Mary (Mrs. Glasgow) died in the early spring
of 1885, and during her mother's absence in Ireland
she had the experience of being left in charge of the
ménage at 13 Rue de Phalsbourg. That she fulfilled
the duties conscientiously is one of several things
indicated by a letter to her friend Ella Martin.
" Do you like keeping accounts? " she asks. " I have
to do that now, and I feel it a great weight on my
shoulders. The first few days after Mama went away
I always woke very early, thinking of all the things I
had to do and my responsibility. Papa has come
home for déjeuner nearly every day. To-morrow he
will have a half-holiday, as it is Mid-Lent (*Mi-carême*).
. . . My china painting does not get on very
quickly now. I missed two lessons while Mama was
away, and will miss another to-morrow. I have been
struggling with my Algebra, and now I am glad to say
it looks more hopeful. . . On Sunday I got a
whole lot of snowdrops from an aunt in Ireland, and
they were very lovely."

Two years later we find that she is still much dis-
satisfied with herself as an occasional " mistress of
the house." In the light of what she afterwards became in that capacity, it is well to recall and record
her early struggles. To a friend she writes : " I look
upon it as a pleasure to write you, but I dare not
allow myself too much of it for fear of neglecting my
duties. My father is very anxious that I should
become a good household manager. I am trying hard

D

to be systematic and orderly, but it is difficult for me, and I waste a lot of time over it."

Meanwhile how does she fare in her spiritual life? Sometimes she finds the battle going against her. It may be true that poets are born, not made, but with saints—to use the New Testament word for Christians —it is otherwise. The eager generalisations which one hears about " the once-born " and " the sky-blue " always seem more than a little hasty. Mary at any rate was one of those who echo Browning's confession, " I find it hard to be a Christian." When she was a young girl, her father and she were walking home from Passy Church one Sunday together. He said something about being good, and she answered, " Well, father, it seems to me the hardest thing in the world to be good." And writing in the last year of her teens, she says to a friend : " As for the temptation to bad temper you complain of, I know very well what it is. It is also my great enemy. Sometimes I feel so dreadfully cross, and then I remember I should pray for help to fight against it and give it up, but I sometimes feel as if I *could* not just then. So often I am beaten and just give in. I wonder how God bears with us at all, we trust Him so little." Of one thing, however, she was confident—that even her failures and lack of faith would not alter God's purpose. " The last verse of Psalm 138 suits me so well. I am sure that although I am so weak and so bad now, ' the Lord *will* perfect that which concerneth me.' Some day I shall be like Him."

Among God's ways of claiming her wholly for Himself, one appeared at the time hard indeed. Her little brother Frank, born on January 10, 1886, was taken away on the last day of June in the following year. As we read the letters she wrote after his death, we feel the beating of a very tender heart. " That dear little face, I see it so plainly, and oh ! I long for it so. But, do you know that I have never loved God so well, nor felt His loving presence so much, as since He took away my wee pet. I had often heard of His being so kind in time of trouble, but have never half believed it. When I felt so lonely after Frankie was away, I used to pray that God would fill the empty place in my heart with His own presence. I don't know what we should have done without His help in these dreadful, dreary days. For myself I shall try to be a kinder sister to the ones left, to show I am thankful to have them. That one small child, we seemed all to have gathered round him so, and he seemed so necessary to us. But our Best Friend has other plans. Perhaps God wants me to do some work for Him, for now He has given me good health and time. If so, I pray that He may show it me plainly and help me. . . . Our dear wee Frankie, our little sunbeam, it is sometimes hard to think it is best that he should be gone. But however much we want him, I dare not wish him back to this sad world. When I am in my unselfish moods, I feel very glad that he will not know anything about the difficulty of serving God, only the delight of it."

To Hélène Wehrlin she wrote about the same time : " Oh ! Hélène, we are much too disposed to think of what we have lost, and not of what our darling has gained. Grandpapa tells us in one of his letters that our little Frank now knows more than the oldest and wisest man on earth, and he is sure that he can now sympathise with us more than we sympathised with him when he suffered. It seems to me that that must make him sorry (if it be possible that he feels the least sorrow) to see us weep so much and long to see him again. . . . But it is hard for us. The house seems so empty even when we are all there. I believe that our dear Saviour makes this emptiness in our hearts that He may fill them Himself. I do not know how I dare to call myself a Christian while I give Him so divided a heart and do so little for Him. Dear Hélène, I have much need of your prayers, that He would let me know what I ought to do."

The work for God which thus began to shape itself vaguely before her mind, was indeed awaiting her, but not in France. All of a sudden her outer life was completely and permanently changed. Ireland, which had hitherto been a mere health and holiday resort, containing such playgrounds as Groomsport, Newcastle, Carnlough, Portrush, and Castlerock, was now to be her home. On a November evening in 1887 she begins a letter to Ella Martin in French : " I am in bed, snugly wrapped up, for it is very cold to-night; " and then she breaks into English : " God is good to me. He gives me so many of my wishes. Can you believe it? It is nearly certain that we are to go and live in Ireland. Papa starts to-morrow morning for Belfast,

and we shall not be quite sure of this till we hear from
him. All this week I have felt in such a state of
excitement. I tried not to wish too vehemently for this
—not to set my heart too much on it—to remember
that God would give us what He knows to be best
for us. But I am weak, and I should be terribly disappointed if it were decided that we are not to go.
Oh ! I pray God that He will make me love *His* will.
And I will not be so faithless as not to believe that
He will answer that prayer."

Before Mary wrote again to the same friend the
matter was settled. Two days after Christmas she
says : " We are very, very busy. I hardly know how
we shall get everything done for the day of our departure. It is fixed for Friday, January 6th. As yet we
are principally occupied with paying farewell visits."
She felt it especially hard to say good-bye to Passy with
all its sacred associations. A new pastor, M. Stapfer,
was just beginning his work there, and he and
Madame Stapfer seemed to be her " ideal of a minister
and his wife—so good, so simple, so sympathetic."
When they called to bid the family adieu, she " could
have cried at the thought of going."

None of Mary's Paris friends felt her approaching
departure so keenly as Hélène. " It was on a
Sunday towards the end of 1887," writes this
comrade, " that after the school lessons were over she
gave me a piece of news which dismayed me, all the
more as our friendship had still further deepened
while we had been engaged in religious work together.
This was nothing less than the announcement that

she and her whole family were going to live in Ireland. 'You will come and see us there,' she said to console me. It was thus that I realised how my dream of visiting Ireland, the fairy-land of my imagination, might after all come true."

The fellowship of Mary and Hélène in Paris, during eleven of the most plastic years of their lives, had been very precious to both. "After I left school," writes the latter, "and went to study elsewhere, we met less often, but our friendship in no way suffered. Once a week, usually on Thursday, I would go to her or she came to me. Often we read English books, but we always talked in French. We did needle-work together, and Mary would play to me the latest pieces of piano music she had been learning. From 1883 to 1887 we met not only to read and work together, but also to play tennis on Thursdays. My friends had a court at Neuilly, and there we often played." Long afterwards Hélène wrote, "Certainly the steadfast friendship which united Mary and me was an influence in my life which I feel more and more as I grow older and look back on the way travelled. A true friendship, such as ours was, is a benediction."

Some remarkable words of Christian assurance are contained in the last letter—as far as appears—which Mary wrote before leaving France. "I don't doubt that I am a Christian. I know I have given myself to Christ and He has accepted me. I know He will not let me perish, otherwise I should not be happy for a moment. I should not be afraid to die this very night; I am sure God would receive me for Jesus' sake, and I should be happy to go and be with Him."

Mary Stuart, sailing from France in her nineteenth year, is said to have expressed her regret in the words :

> Adieu, O pleasant land of France,
> That nursed my happy infancy !
> Beloved home of sweet romance,
> Adieu ! to leave thee is to die.*

Our Irish Mary did not feel the parting quite so keenly as that. Dearly she, too, loved the fair land and the splendid capital in which all her earliest, formative years were spent. She grew from childhood to youth, from youth to womanhood, on the banks of the Seine. Every boulevard and avenue became familiar ground to her. Daily she breathed the air, watched the crowds, studied the life of the city which gives the laws of taste and fashion to the world. She attended a French school and had French tutors in her home. She spoke the French language so perfectly that she continued to think in it as long as she lived. She acquired an indefinable piquancy of manner and precision of speech which were markedly Parisian. But the fact remains that Paris never dazzled her eyes or captured her heart. The facile maxim about doing in Rome as the Romans do had no force or meaning for

---

* I give but a rough rendering of Béranger's exquisite lines—
> Adieu, charmant pays de France
> Que je dois tant chérir !
> Berceau de mon heureux enfance,
> Adieu ! te quitter c'est mourir.

her. Even as a young girl she displayed a rare independence of spirit, friendly and yet aloof, pliant in the " little nothings," but immovable as a rock in all the deeper things. The gay Parisians, some of whom spoke of her with genuine admiration as " the Puritan maiden," knew well that she had no real kinship of thought or feeling with themselves. They recognised that she was a stranger in the midst of their Vanity Fair. Not that she was blind to the glitter and glamour of the passing show. There is a heart-cry in her frequent prayer, " Oh, that God would keep me out of this great worldliness ! " Her prayer was answered. Protected by the countercharm of the higher life, she was in the world without being of it. And as she began, so she continued. No one ever questioned her deep heart-love of Ireland, yet nobody ever thought of her as typically Irish. Least of all had she the airs of " a citizen of the world," though her outlook became astonishingly wide. No words describe a high patriotism like hers but " My kingdom is not of this world." One of her earliest friends remembers how wistfully she used to sing as a young girl :

> " Une belle Patrie dans les haux cieux
> Rassemble après la vie les bien-heureux."

That was her only real *Patrie*—the whole spiritual realm of the King of Love.

CHAPTER III

THE FLOWER OF WOMANHOOD

MARY'S life in Ireland began a week before her twenty-first birthday.   On the first Saturday of 1888 she had a rough crossing of St. George's Channel, and on the second she passed the mystic line between girlhood and womanhood.   Her earnest spirit made this juncture an occasion for looking before and after, still more for looking within, where her anxious thoughts troubled her and her tender conscience humbled her.   That divine discontent which springs from much communion with Christ was at this time peculiarly strong in her.   She suffered from " the malady of the ideal." Her Sunday meditations on the morrow of her birthday left her anything but complacent.   " I have not attained " is the burden of a letter written in the evening, apparently the first of her Irish letters.   " I have just been reading *Like Christ,*"* she says, " and the effect it has had on me is to make me feel, even more

* One of Dr. Andrew Murray's books.

than I have been doing of late, my weakness and my
wickedness and my want of almost everything resemb-
ling a Christian life. I find a description of myself—
' they know their own weakness, and count
walking like Christ an impossibility.' That is just
what I was thinking yesterday morning in bed.
I felt my weakness so much that I was sure I should
fall; I had a sort of presentiment that something would
soon happen, to show to all interested in me that my
religion was really nothing—a sham. I knew I was
too weak to walk with Jesus and like Him. But then,
how good God was to me; He said to me, ' I, the Lord
thy God, will hold thy right hand, saying unto thee,
Fear not, I will help thee.' I of myself could not
promise to keep close to Jesus, but if He holds my
hand, if He helps me, I will not be afraid, I *will* not;
I *will* trust Him and praise Him.''

By this time she had reached a woman's intuitive
judgment, from which she was never to recede, that
the presence or absence of Christ in human life makes
all the difference between optimism and pessimism.
'' The more,'' she writes, '' I look at my dear Lord,
the more I love Him, and (what I discover again
and again, and forget again and again when I am
careless and indifferent) it is only when looking to
Him and trusting Him that I am happy, but *then* I
am happy, *so* happy. He is so good to me and makes
me see so much good in life; at other times I feel inclined to be a pessimist and say, Is life worth living? ''

She had left in Paris not only the friends of her
childhood—Hélène Wehrlin and Emma Thomas were

specially dear—but the Church whose life and work had so greatly interested her. New friends in Ireland just on trial, and new work might be long in coming to her hands. For months she felt very lonely. She had no sister, and much as her brothers loved her they were too young to enter into her inner life. Writing towards the end of May to Ella Martin, she says : " Many times of late I have wanted, oh ! wanted so badly, someone to talk to, someone to help me to be good. It seems to me God does not let me have my friends just when I want them most, and it has occurred to me perhaps this is so that I may let Him alone satisfy my longing."

This idea of human friendship, as of a cup put to her lips and then withdrawn, in order to be replaced by the chalice of Divine love, recurs frequently in her youthful letters. If we may all be known by our favourite words, " the Best Friend " is a phrase which peculiarly reveals her. Looking back at a later time, with a wider experience of the Christian life, she wrote : " I remember so well wishing years ago for friends of the kind I have now, who could speak to me of God and help me, and I had not the courage or was too ignorant to begin myself; but I believe this very thing, this very solitude, was a blessing of God; it led me in a kind of despair to seek sympathy, help, guidance, teaching, all, from Him alone. I am sure it was this that made me always think of the Lord Jesus as a Friend. I am sure that otherwise I should have trusted more in earthly friends

and less in Him. I thank God for this among the
many, many blessings He has given me.''

Along with her desire for friends there went the
longing for work.   Holding that everyone is " sent
from God " with some special task to fulfil, she felt
that she would not be truly living until she definitely
knew His will regarding herself.   On her third Sunday
in Belfast she writes : " I have been reading the Song
of Songs and liked it awfully.   Look at the end of
chap. iv.   I would like to be as this garden, well-
watered, producing fruit for Him who loves me.   I
am sure that if I used some of the mercies He gives
me to help those who have not so many, my life would
be more like this watered garden.''   She began to study
the calls received by Servants of God, and on a Sunday
evening in April we find her writing : " You ask what
I think of Jeremiah?   The first chapter interested,
touched, and moved me very much.   Is it not a
wonderful story—this conversation between God and
Jeremiah?   The latter seems so taken by surprise
that God expects such great things of him, and he is
asked to have such strong faith in God !   That was a
hard commission given him.   Oh ! how I can understand his timidity at first.   But that is a good word
God says to him, ' Be not afraid of their faces, for I
am with thee to deliver thee.'   I am sure this is the
great cause of all our fears and timidity in His service,
that we forget that God is really with us, close beside
us.   We (that is I) mostly believe it as an abstract
fact, but not as a reality.   And yet that statement is
repeated again and again in the Bible ; I have just

been coming across it very often of late. That is the comfort, strength, reassuring, in fact all, that we need. . . . I do want to glorify God in my life. I have been thinking a great deal about that of late, indeed for some time past. I pray God, if it be His will, to show me some way in which I can work definitely for Him, something special. Ask that I may have grace given me to follow just where He leads."

In the same letter Mary tells how she has been reading her grandfather's book on the Apocalypse. She wonders why God has given us part of His word in such a strange form. " Perhaps it is to make us think. The first few chapters are easy enough. They have always had a great interest for me. Some parts have frightened me very much. ' I know thy works, that thou hast a name that thou livest and art dead.' I daresay you understand my feelings in wondering if that was meant for me. But I will not give way to this. I am sure I am Jesus Christ's and He will keep me. ' I will trust and not be afraid.' I have often thought too about having left my first love. But I am sure that is not so. I never loved my Best Friend so much as now, and every day He teaches me to know Him better, which means of course loving Him better."

Meanwhile her heart was still often in Paris. Even the perfume of a sprig of mimosa, sent by Hélène on her birthday, had power, she confesses, to " Parisianise " her at once again. Letters which she received from Passy Church girls, whom she had helped to lead to Christ, filled her heart with gratitude. One of them signs herself " Your old and ever devoted pupil," and another " Your scholar who loves you tenderly." And Mary could not but be deeply touched when M. Moret wrote to her, some months after she left Paris, as follows : " I will confess to you, my dear child, that I begin to find the time long, and there is nothing in that which need astonish you, for you were my favourite pupil (*mon élève preférée*), and the satisfaction which you always gave me has made me very sensible of your departure : add to that the void which your absence has made in my musical *réunions* ! Happily there remains with me the memory of the eight good years during which you were entrusted to my care, along with the praises which I daily receive regarding you. And I do not doubt that you are as happy in your own *patrie* as you were in mine."

At times she seemed to question whether she was indeed as happy as she had been, and though she could not see forward she was tempted to doubt and fear. Time alone would tell whether she was to find in Ireland the contentment her spirit sighed for. Two years, in reality, had yet to run before she was to receive her clear call to " something special " and find complete happiness in answering it. And in the interval she was tried, as gold is tried, in the fire. The essaying of her art was a small matter in comparison with the testing of her spiritual womanhood. She was to realise in practice as well as in theory that the adventure of life is fraught with infinite possibilities of both good and evil. Her days of probation were days of peril in which she was conscious of fighting a battle that must end in victory or defeat. Happily she was always alive to the deceitful lure of false ideals. " Pray for me," she wrote to Hélène, " if you desire my happiness, but do not pray that all my wishes may be granted, for some of them, I am sure, would do me no good. Leave that to our kind Father, who knows much better than you and I what is for our good and His glory."

Mary came to Ireland at a time when Christian men and women had still somewhat hazy ideas regarding the relation of religion to art in general and music in particular. The question of the use of organs and hymns in public worship was the subject of all-night debates in the General Assembly of the Church of her fathers. She very soon found herself surrounded by dear Christian women—wives and daughters, it might be, of Assembly debaters—who were conscientiously opposed not only to instrumental music in Churches but to musical " performances " of every sort. If they were right, the years which she had spent in studying her beloved masters of classical music had been wasted. The idea was little short of sacrilege, yet she listened patiently to the arguments of opponents, and replied with perfect courtesy. She was slow to speak, but her few, calm words were often wonderfully effective.

She was invited to attend a " Bible Talk " of ladies on the subject of " Amusements, where to draw the line." Fifteen were present, and this is her brief account of the proceedings. " There was nothing new. Miss X expressed herself very strongly. She disapproves of concerts and thinks practising a waste of time. You would be better employed singing in the slums. I think she surely has no musical talent. I disagree with her. . . . When I was studying the subject I could find in the Bible nothing except Job's praying for his children when they were feasting. This shows possible danger when people get absorbed in amusements. The fourth Commandment and other passages speak of Work and Rest, only those two. So I think in so far as amusements are rest they are right. Dancing for six to eight hours is no rest. Unselfishness and thought for others should be our rule; Christ at the supper of Cana gives us an example of doing all we can for the enjoyment of others. I aired all these opinions, and felt very brave in speaking so much. . . . Another lady condemned Bazaars. I said nothing, but listened to her flood of eloquence—she *can* talk. But you know the principle of Bazaars is good. It is—How shall I get money to give to God's work? I will make something and sell it. Nearly everything good in itself can be and is perverted."

Happily there were already not a few in the Church who wished to see all arts, especially music, devoted to the service of Him who implanted the love of them in the hearts of His children. Apart, however, from the primary question whether a place is to be found. for classical music in the Christian scheme of things, there is the secondary one of artistic skill to produce it. *I may* is one thing, *I can* is another. Thirty years ago there were not many Irish pianists who were capable of interpreting Beethoven and Mozart, Bach and Brahms, Chopin and Liszt. That was what Mary very unostentatiously began to do. " I well remember," says a true lover of music,* " the first time I heard her play and the impression she made on me as a brilliant pianist. In those days I was frequently out at musical entertainments, and I can safely say that she was undoubtedly the most accomplished amateur pianist in Belfast at that time. She could play the most difficult music with ease, and no singer could wish for a more sympathetic accompanist. She was a born musician, and yet so unassuming that to anyone who had not previously heard her play her brilliancy came as a pleasant surprise as soon as her fingers touched the keys. But indeed it might be said with truth that this was a characteristic of all her work."

M. Moret's pupil had little desire to shine in what are called musical circles. She was free from personal ambition, while she coveted earnestly the best gifts. Taught to repeat daily certain great words about God's kingdom and power and glory, she felt that any use of talents without direct regard to His will is, however disguised, but a form of self-idolatry. If she wished to give pleasure to others, she must first make sure that she was not seeking her own honour but her Master's. She used to tell what a power over her mind lay in her father's great expression and rule of

* Rev. Edward Clarke M.A., Strabane.

E

life, " It—is—my—duty." And she found that if
there was any conflict of motives and ideals in her
heart, she never prayed for guidance in vain. She
read no book of poems with more delight than *The
Idylls of the King,* and Guinevere's finest words came
to her not with the poignancy of regret but with the
radiance of hope, " We needs must love the highest
when we see it."

M. Moret had given his pupil his highest word of
praise when he said she had " the sacred fire " (*le feu
sacré*). Belfast was not slow to discover her genius,
nor backward in providing occasions for its display.
Display was the last word she cared to use regarding
anything she ever did, but she put her gifts at the
service of every good cause, and she joined a society
called the Lorelei, which attracted the best musical
talent of the city.

At first she could not help being amused when she
discovered that to not a few of her audiences she gave a
new conception of piano-playing. " Here," she wrote
to Hélène, "everybody sings at amateur concerts, which
are numerous, and there is little but singing in drawing-
rooms. People scarcely ever listen when the piano
is played—rather they talk the louder—but they are
silent for the singing." Clearly some things needed
to be changed. A real pianist's sitting down to play
is not a signal for more animated conversation.
Rather the touch of the keys is like the waving of a
magician's wand, making a stillness in which soul
speaks to soul.

Mary's letters to Hélène now begin to convey many

little items of news like the following : " On Friday
there was a Concert in Elmwood Schoolroom, given by
the Musical Association, which Alek and I joined a fortnight ago. A Cantata of Sullivan's was given and
went very well. I accompanied both the choruses
and the solos." . . . " At the Lorelei Maude
MacBride and I played a Symphony of Mozart, and I
had to contribute in addition a Melody and a Tarantelle of Rubenstein." . . . " This evening we have
a Concert at Windsor, where I am to play the
Harmonious Blacksmith." . . . " To-morrow we
go to a Sale for Missions at Mr. Park's Church. I
have to play. Here it is the custom to provide music at
Sales for those who wish to listen." . . . " I don't
like to refuse when I am asked. The other day I
played at a Concert on behalf of a Hospital." . . .
" The Lorelei Concert took place on Tuesday. Brahms
and Bach were the composers. I played a *finale* of
the Sonatas of Brahms; it was very difficult and I
had only a few hours to study it." . . . " Ina* and I
played the Second Rhapsodie of Liszt as a duet. It
is truly a magnificent piece. I was happy because I
found we played very well together." . . . " On
Saturday I have to play at an evening concert for
Working People, got up by the Temperance League.
I don't know how it is that the Ulster Hall fills me
with such a special horror. I suppose it is the size
of the place and the memory of artistes whom I have
heard there."

Mary played invariably without the musical score,

*Her cousin Alexandrina Huston, now Mrs. Hamilton Martin.

but she seemed never to make mistakes or be in any way flurried. Alike in the grace of slow movements and the verve of rapid passages her execution was flawless. Only once, at a Lorelei concert, do we hear of her experiencing difficulties. " I got into a muddle," she confesses in a letter. " I recovered myself, got very frightened again, turned up my music which was happily in front of me, and so got safe to the end. I believe I received more congratulations that time than I ever did before. Papa told me he had inwardly said ' Bravo, Mary.' He thought I acted in a very composed manner, not even frowning. He little knew the disturbance there was inside." She adds the remarkable circumstance that, when driving to the place where she was to play, she had mentally rehearsed her contribution note by note— significant of her careful study and accurate know- ledge—and that her memory had failed her at the very point where she subsequently broke down.

She loved best to play, not in the excitement of the concert-room, but in the quiet of her own or a friend's home, with perhaps only one or two listeners. It was then that she could give fullest expression to her own emotions. In the summer of her first year in Ireland Hélène Wehrlin came over from France to spend some weeks with her at Mount Randal, and the letters they afterwards exchanged show that it had been their delight, at the end of a day's experiences, to sit and play in the twilight (*dans le crépuscule*), sometimes together (*à quatre mains*), and sometimes the one to the other. Like the true music-lover she was, Mary liked to listen even better than to play, and good music always " found " her in the deepest part of her being. How suggestive is the following little note, written in the midsummer of 1890 : " Yesterday Papa, Nita and I sat in the twilight in the drawing-room window while Nellie* played some beautiful music. As I sat there with my eyes shut I felt so, so happy. The music chimed in so beautifully with my thankfulness to God for all His mercies, and the Lord Jesus seemed very near."

The best appreciation of Mary's playing is contributed by her friend Mrs. Walker, *née* Maude MacBride. " Her intense love of music was the first bond that drew us together as girls. I remember well the first time I heard her play after the family came to Belfast to live. She was staying with us at Portrush, and I, who was several years her junior, was rather in awe of this somewhat reserved and austere young girl. However, she was requested to play, and after she had finished her first piece, which was Mendelssohn's *Bees' Wedding,* I became her devoted and even passionate admirer. She was a different being at the piano. Her long, beautifully-formed fingers flew over the notes with such delicacy and precision, and such intense feeling was in her every sway of her body and inclination of her dainty head, that she seemed the very spirit of music, and she always moved her audience, whether to sadness or gaiety. She never failed to touch them. I have known many musical people, professional and other-

* Mary Helen Huston, now Mrs. John Harris.

wise, but I have never known anyone except Mary, who put so much of her own charming personality into everything she played. . . . As girls we belonged to the same musical society, and she and I met every day or two to practise duets together. It was in hours like these that the gaiety of her nature showed itself. Those people who thought her very staid and serious (and there were many) would have been surprised indeed had they heard her merry peals of laughter when we came down with all four hands on wrong notes, or when we found our ideas of rhythm widely divergent! When she married she had, of necessity, less time for music; but every time I went to stay with her, it all revived again, and for hours she would hold me spell-bound, while she roamed from one Composer to another, entirely without notes, her wonderful musical memory never failing her even in the most difficult and longest of Beethoven's sonatas. . . . Well, she and her beautiful talent are gone from here, but to me she lives, and it only needs one bar of the music she loved and played to conjure up her graceful form as she bent lovingly, nay, even caressingly, over her piano."

It will not be imagined that music was ever Mary's sole interest. She had many things on hand when she wrote to Hélène, " *Je suis* busy, busy, busy," and told her in another letter that time was passing with a *vélocipèdité incommensurable!* She became a teacher in Windsor Sunday School, and very carefully prepared for every lesson. She was as fond as ever of sketching and

STUDY OF HOLLYHOCKS.   BY MARY CRAWFORD.

painting. She began to teach herself Greek, with one or other of her brothers to aid her, and ere long she had the satisfaction of reading part of the Book of Revelation with her venerable grandfather in the original. " Some days," she says, " it (Greek) seems dreadfully hard, but on others it goes swimmingly." No mention is made meanwhile of works of fiction, but she had more serious and no less delightful books to read. " I greatly like Bacon's *Essays,* Carlyle's *Hero-worship,* Holmes' *Autocrat of the Breakfast Table,* and Green's *History of the English People.*" She attended a dozen University extension lectures on Shakespeare, while on Monday afternoons she and Maude MacBride met to read Schiller's *Don Carlos.* " We are also supposed," Mary remarks, " to talk in French or German, but that doesn't always come off."

The width of her interests is indicated by the following note to Hélène : " This week we are having a course of lectures—one almost every day—by Dr. George Macdonald. They are really admirable. He becomes impassioned over his theme and carries one away with him. It is necessary to be at the lecture room half an hour before the time in order to get a good place. He has already spoken of Robert Burns, Tennyson, and Hamlet. The last was magnificent. He has still Wordsworth and Dante. Ever since there was a question of his coming, everybody has been talking of him and reading his books. I hope to re-read all the works on which he has commented, in order to re-discover the beauties and do something for my education on that side. . . . On Monday

H. M. Stanley appeared in the Ulster Hall, so that I think we have had almost enough of lectures for one week."

The most important of all her pursuits in those crowded days is alluded to by one of her friends. "When I first knew Mary (about 1890) she was taking a course of Bible studies in connection with a College by Post, and this three years' course she succeeded in getting me to undertake also. Her study of the Bible was intense and earnest, and she would speak of having read the book of Isaiah or Jeremiah or some other prophet, and would be quite willing to give her opinion of the writer and his book."

Her quest of sacred knowledge was never a task-work, because she had a genuine love of the subject. After preparation for a Bible lesson which she was about to give, she says : "The passage is Col. i. 9-13. There is a great deal in it, and it is wonderfully beautiful. I like very much what there is in Ephesians, Colossians, and 2 Peter, all in their first chapters respectively, about *knowledge*. I like so much the idea of growing in the knowledge of God and of His will, of Jesus, of His word, and of all His wonderful works." Clearly she is on the way to the highest and finest Bible scholarship, for what Browning says of Art holds equally good of Divinity, the quest of which is stimulated by

> the rage
> Of knowing the absolute truth of things,
> For truth's sake whole and sole.

At the same time there was no lessening of Mary's love of music, and she embraced every opportunity she had of hearing sacred masterpieces. With two Belfast friends, Miss Janie Craig* and her brother, she went to London to attend the centennial Handel Festival at the Crystal Palace. " It was indeed a magnificent spectacle," she wrote to Hélène, " that choir which seemed to line all the high wall before us. With the orchestra there are 4,000 executants, and it is marvellous to see how they all follow the least movement of the conductor, who seems so small down below. Of the music I do not speak; it is useless, it is impossible, at least for me, to give any idea of it. But you know how greatly I admire Handel. At six o'clock it was all over, and after refreshing ourselves with tea (for even with the grandest music one gets hungry!) we took a walk round the Gardens before returning."

When Paderewski came to Belfast, she of course attended his concert. " It is a kind of music lesson," she said, " a very superior kind, to hear a man like that play." In the Ulster Hall he thrilled her by his rendering of one of her own favourite pieces, a Concerto of Chopin. She and her brother James were sitting in different parts of the Hall, and at the end they met in the vestibule. The same thought was in both their minds, and they expressed it simultaneously. " Mary, you never played that Concerto of Chopin ! "

* Now Secretary of the Women's Missionary Association of the English Presbyterian Church.

" Jemmy, I never knew how to play that Concerto of Chopin ! "

In that busy time Mary found that if she was to love the highest she had a battle to fight. For the highest is neither music, nor art, nor literature, but the service of Christ. " Dear Hélène," we find her writing, " I understand so well what you say about letting the little occupations steal away your time and thoughts from higher things. Again and again has this happened to me, and I have grown cold; heavenly things have lost their interest, and I have been miserable. Again and again with untiring patience my heavenly Father has received me back. I am amazed at His kindness. Every day I become more and more persuaded of the necessity of giving nourishment to our soul if we want it to be in health. No wonder that it languishes if we starve or half starve it."

Mary and Hélène were both very human, and their correspondence after the latter's visit to Ireland gives the clearest possible idea how the Christ of to-day moulds His saints—His whole-hearted servants and supremely happy friends. It describes that " temptation in the wilderness " which comes in one form or another to every earnest spirit—the closest involuntary contact with a world that knows not God, and the swift renunciation of it in a rush of devotion to a Master who, though unseen, is loved in every fibre of one's being.

" You remember," Mary says in one letter, " that

Sunday evening when Mr. Ferris pr ached a sermon that roused us both so : well, it made me begin to think, and I awoke to the fact that I was getting very much buried in worldly things, that my heavenly Father was getting far from me, that my idea of taking up my Sunday class was distasteful to me. I found that if I did not take care I should become much too fond of worldly pleasures—it made me think of the parable of the Sower, and the thorns growing up and choking the good seed. Oh ! how weak I felt, as if I could not fight against such strong enemies. I was forgetting that ' He that is for us is stronger than those who are against us.' Sometimes it is true I did think of this, and then I found I did not want to give up anything that was pleasant but hurtful. And yet I *did* and *do* want to belong altogether to Christ, to live in communion with Him. I cannot tell you what a battle was raging in me; it made me think of ' the law in my members warring against the law of my mind,' that Paul speaks of. But God, in His goodness, as always, answered our prayers, gave me back His peace, showed me how strong He is to keep me right in any circumstances, showed me that I must count it all joy when I fall into manifold temptations, taught me once more to say, ' In Thee, O Lord, do I put my trust.' I think God let me see my great weakness to teach me that of myself I can do nothing. I thank God from my heart for teaching me this.''

In a second letter Mary says, " We very greatly need help from on high to walk straight.

One day, when I was much troubled, Papa read out of Hebrews xi., and those words, ' He endured as seeing Him who is invisible,' came to me as a very message from heaven. That is the only way I can endure. Oh ! how sorry I am for those who cannot see Him. So often I have just to fly into His arms for comfort and refuge from the distracting and distressing thoughts and events that surround me. It is good to remember how ' all things work together for good to them that love Him.' "

In a third letter Mary takes her friend to the burning centre of things. She gives her a precious page of autobiography. She goes back in spirit to her Bethel—her garden in the valley between Sèvres and Ville d'Avray—where she sought the Lord and found Him, and vowed that if He spared her life she would serve Him for ever. " Do you remember," she asks, " telling me once that you found me looking younger and more cheerful (*rajeunie et plus gaie*) for a time back? Well, this happier period of my life corresponds exactly to that of my Christian life. I confess to you that it was fear, the fear of death when I was ill, that first drove me (*m'a poussée*) to seek the protection of Jesus Christ. At the beginning I scarcely believed that He had really accepted me, and that He would surely defend me against evil of every kind, and from the fears to which I was so subject. But now I am gradually discovering, what I have often heard without understanding it, and almost without even believing it, that the presence of my Saviour at my side and His love can make me more light of heart than anyone ever

feels who has not these things. Every hour of my life
I see more clearly that it is only the children of God
who are happy, and He gives them joy in no matter
what situation they find themselves.''

Hélène's heart made glad response. In simple
language she, too, recalls the most momentous fact in
her life. '' It was you, dear Mary,'' she writes, '' who
led me to that God whom I was serving in mere form
(*en pure forme*). I thirsted for something, and at last
I found that what I lacked was faith. And now that
we are united by faith, may nothing ever separate us !
God forgive us, and guide us, and grant that we may
be re-united for ever.''

'' My old friends pen and paper '' is an arresting
phrase which Mary uses in one of those letters. '' I am
too stupid to *speak* of these things, but I can *write* of
them as much as you would like, my heart is so full.''
And there is nothing in the world that Hélène desires
more than that her friend should just go on writing out
of the fulness of her heart. '' Pen and paper '' have
become *old* friends to Mary very early in life. Some
day others besides Hélène may discover that she is one
of those who love to use the pen as many a man, but
no woman, loves to use the sword, and fortunately we
live in a world in which the good done with the one
weapon is even greater—which is saying something
tremendous—than the evil done with the other.

Mary now began to find in Ireland the
intimate friends of her own sex for whom
she had been longing. After ten years in
Western America her cousin Susan Horner re-

visited the homeland, and of her Mary writes: "She was the heroine of my childhood, but I have changed so much since then, and letters are so unsatisfactory, that I hardly knew what I would think of her when she came back. Well, she has come almost unexpectedly, and it was just lovely when she and I were together. She has done me a world of good. First, she is so merry, I don't see how anyone could be ill in the house with her, if it be true that ' a merry heart doeth good like medicine.' Second, she is so good, in such a modest unassuming way; we have just been constantly finding out her goodnesses and kindnesses almost by chance, and she thinks nothing of herself. I shall not go on to thirdly, fourthly, fifthly—it would be interminable. She is apt to hide her light under a bushel in company, and she greatly dislikes parties, but otherwise she has, it seems to me, every good quality."

Another friend who had a great influence over Mary was her father's sister Annie, the youngest of the large Maine Mount family. "I remember," Mary writes, "I used to think my Aunts Olivia and Annie kind of perfections who could never understand troubles and difficulties and weaknesses like mine; but by speaking with them I find they understand right well from experience, and for this I love them all the more." Aunt Annie, who married the Rev. J. B. Huston, her father's successor at Randalstown, was a woman of fine public spirit, a telling speaker who advocated many good causes, especially temperance. It was her personal charm, however, that captivated her niece.

" Each time I see her," Mary writes, " I love her more and more. I am glad I am getting more courageous in the talking way—about spiritual things I mean. We had some delightful talks together, and I got light on many of my ideas and difficulties from her. Truly God is wonderfully good to give me so many and such dear friends. She has a thousand cares, great and small, of her own, but that does not prevent her from being always ready to talk of whatever interests you and whatever worries you. I have spoken to her about many things in the Bible which used to torment me, and she has explained everything to me so well. I am afraid of many people, but of her not at all."

Soon after this was written, Mr. Huston died very suddenly while on a visit to Mount Randal. The event made a profound impression on Mary's mind. " Aunt Annie," she says, " through it all was wonderful. We looked at her and praised and thanked the Lord. She is a most beautiful example of Christ's power to comfort and sustain. I could not help uttering a word of admiration for her, and she just said, ' It's not me.' And truly it is not herself. No human being alone could act as she does. God has been letting us see what is ' the exceeding greatness of His power towards us who believe.' She told me the one thing she had asked for was that she should have some word of testimony from her husband that he was at peace. You know he was nearly unconscious all the time and hardly spoke a word. And she heard him say, near the end, ' Underneath are the everlasting arms.' Then she said she could just praise God and sing to Him in her heart. Ina, dear child, had an ordeal, going home alone to break the news. She went away so bravely."

If Mary had not yet found her life-work, it had at least become quite clear that art for art's sake would never satisfy her. Another letter to Hélène runs thus : " I have lately played at two concerts. Every time the hour comes for going to a concert, I am so unhappy that I promise never again to play in public, and yet when I am again asked I say Yes." That could scarcely continue, and we are not surprised to find her saying to the same confidante : " The only thing for us to do is to give ourselves entirely into our Master's keeping, and He will care for us most tenderly. Hélène dear, let us pray that God would teach us to understand His love better, teach us to be satisfied with it, teach us to devote our lives to His service. I thank Him that He has showed me many times the emptiness of this world's pleasures. He has given us hearts that need God."

To Hélène she says in another letter : " I admire the philosophical way in which you speak of dancing; we are almost of the same opinion on that subject. You know that I don't dance any longer, and I don't miss it at all. We are here now in the grand season of dancing parties, and for the most part I am not asked to them, though I still receive some invitations. The mere sight of the words ' 8 to 1.30 o'clock,' the bare idea of dancing for five or six hours, fatigues me. I should see in imagination the day after the dance, which is for me always so miserable." She then adds, with some irony, that while she has escaped that particular weariness, another is almost as menacing. " The visits which we ought to pay accumulate astonishingly, and people have many reproaches to make on that score. But one cannot kill oneself ! "

In answer to another friend, cast down by " want of interest and enjoyment " in life, she wrote about the same time : " I know I have often passed through times like that myself. I remember times when the only part of the Bible I cared to read was Ecclesiastes; it seemed to express so well a weariness of everything. I think God allows us to feel that way sometimes, to teach us that nothing in the world can satisfy us—to teach us to say truly, ' Whom have I in heaven but Thee? and there is none upon earth whom I desire beside Thee.' I think the human heart is made to have a great longing which cannot be satisfied when it is not very near to God. I believe that what we want is, so to say, to make the acquaintance (*de faire la connaissance*) of the Lord Jesus, to make of Him a friend, and learn to know Him as one learns to know a friend; to speak to Him at every moment, about everything, and to read His Word as a letter which He has written to us. And if we keep His friendship, we must try to do *everything* that He has told us."

She tells about the same time how some words she has been reading in Ruskin have chimed in completely with her own thoughts—" by the self-denial of delight, to gain greater delight." At Christmas, 1891, she received from Miss Craig a card with the words, " He

F

will keep the feet of His saints." Of this she wrote,
" It brought back to me the shrinking I used to have
from appropriating promises made to saints, until I
came across the definition of ' saints ' given in Psalm
50, ' they that have made a covenant with Me by
sacrifice.' You and I have certainly done that."

Her " self-denial " is partly described in a letter to
Hélène, written in February, 1892. " At the beginning of this winter I said to myself, that I must
arrange my life so as not to have to go to
all sorts of parties, visits and meetings,
which at one time I thought indispensable. And
already things are going much better. A life always
among other people (en l'air) does not suit me."
Then some elements of the " greater delight " are
enumerated with evident satisfaction : first, she now has
more leisure for reading; second, her health is greatly
improved; and third, she is playing tennis more
vigorously than ever, in winter on the cinder court.

It was always her habit to stop and think, and not
to go on automatically in a groove. She felt the
truth of the old saying that an unexamined life is not
worth living, and her self-scrutinies are never lacking
in severity. In the autumn of 1892, during Mr. D. L.
Moody's last visit to Ireland, we find her judging herself for missing opportunities of well-doing, and especially for failures to confess Christ. " His meetings,"
she writes, " and how he exhorted all to confess Him,
made me feel worse. I was quite excited and miserable about it. The word that began to set me right
again was in Psalm 85, which we sang last Sunday,

our Communion day—'Peace, and turn no more to ill.'* That was the message I got. At first it seemed both comfort and the opposite. I wished it had stopped at Peace, but it didn't, and I believe God is giving me grace once more to leave all my badness with Jesus and start afresh, trusting only in Him. Do you have times when all your unworthiness seems specially opened up and shown to you, your weakness and all? I have them periodically, about once a year, I think. This is certainly one time. Always afterwards He seems as it were to take pains to show me I am forgiven, by making well-doing easier than usual, and helping me to speak, and giving me opportunities again when I felt I nevermore deserved to get any."

Apart from certain critical difficulties which every thoughtful reader of Scripture feels for a time, it does not appear that Mary was ever vexed with any religious doubts. She knew that some who had the will to believe found faith difficult. She could sympathise with them, help them, pray with them and for them, but her own trials were of a different order. One of her young friends, who was destined to be a soul-winner in the Far East, on being asked along with others to name subjects regarding which prayers were desired, made answer, "For myself, that I may be kept from doubting the truth of Christianity." The incident greatly impressed Mary. "Poor girl," she wrote to Hélène, "how I feel for her. It made me

* The words are found in the *The Irish Revision of the Metrical Psalms.*

thank God from the depths of my heart that I have never been troubled on that side. It is not of Jesus Christ that I am tempted to doubt, it is of myself."

Meantime evidences are not wanting that she was quietly and unconsciously radiating the light and warmth of a Christian life upon others, especially those whom she loved most dearly. Writing to a friend on a Sunday evening, she says : " I fully agree with all you say about God's goodness. If your ' cup runneth over ' so does mine. Papa and I had a little conversation to-night while the others were at supper. I don't know how we both came to speak of how happy our lives were; neither of us, we felt, had ever been so happy as now. No mention was there of Christ, yet He was in the thoughts of both. I said I often felt selfish for doing so little to spread the knowledge of what gave me so much happiness. ' You do a good deal,' said my dear father. ' Not much,' said I. ' Oh, yes; to begin with there's the influence you exert at home.' I felt like crying for happiness. Is it possible God has allowed me to exert any influence on my brothers? How unworthy I feel. I cannot fathom my Heavenly Father's kindness in so many ways, in giving me, for instance, such a kind earthly father, and in giving me such encouragements."

One of the best ways in which she influenced her brothers is indicated by another letter to the same friend. " Did I ever tell you about a little meeting which the boys and I, just we five, have on Sunday morning at eight o'clock, before breakfast, for half an hour? We repeat verses we have learned during the week. We are at Ephesians; it is a beautiful portion, and we are getting to understand it much better by learning it by heart. Then some of us, or all in turn, pray for three things—the services of the day, the Sunday School, and Missions. Alek was delighted when I suggested the idea, and I think it does all good. I felt very much inclined not to propose it for fear we should grow cold and formal. But I thought I should be able to trust God with that part of it. And it has gone on well." Whole epistles of the New Testament were thus gradually learned by heart. And among all the sacred memories cherished by four brothers, whose lots in life have been cast in lands so far apart as Ireland, France, India and China, none is more precious than that of the quiet half hours—real moments on the Mount— in which their sister taught them how to be in the Spirit on the Lord's Day.

CHAPTER IV

THE KINGDOM OF GOD

IN the year 1890 the Presbyterian Church in Ireland celebrated the Jubilee of its Indian Mission. In the same year Mary Crawford received her definite and, she never doubted, Divine call to devote her life to the cause of Foreign Missions. She read Robert Jeffrey's *History* of the Mission, which is dedicated jointly to the memory of Dr. William Fleming Stevenson, and to her grandfather, Dr. James Glasgow, "the Church's First Foreign Missionary, and the only Survivor of the Pioneer Band who, fifty years ago, went out to lay the Foundation of the Church's present splendid Indian Mission." As she read on and on, she became conscious of "sensations sweet felt in the blood and felt along the heart." She awoke to the fact that the wonderful story was in a real sense her own. Dear ancestral voices, proclaiming the glory of Christ's Kingdom among the heathen, stirred loud echoes in her soul. The spirit of Anna

86

Gardner and Mary Wightman, who consented to follow Christ whithersoever He should lead them, was her own spirit. Deep called unto deep, and all the enthusiasm of her nature rushed like a torrent into one clear-cut channel. She responded to the summons of the highest ideal, and the love of Foreign Missions became her ruling passion. It was not so much that she took possession of the central truth of her religion, as that the truth, infinitely greater than herself, came down upon her and bore her away a willing captive, dedicated in spirit to a lifelong service.

Christianity, rightly understood, can never foster a self-centred life. If its first principle is the ever-coming Kingdom of God, it is not only unselfish but heroic. It calls for heroic thinking as well as acting. The very grandeur of the ideals it stands for makes them difficult to grasp. In one of the letters which Mary wrote in that memorable Jubilee year, she says : "This morning when I knelt to pray, my first impulse was to begin, 'Keep me from temptation,' when suddenly I remembered that that is not where the Lord told us to begin; that only comes in the middle. I remembered that even our seemingly holy wishes may be for our own glory, and I suspected that first petition of mine of being rather for my glory. I am sure the desire is very predominant with me to be thought good by my family and friends and the world in general. Then I remembered how the Lord told us to begin, 'Hallowed be Thy name.' It seemed to me that in my prayer I should try to realise that wish first—that He might be exalted though I be less thought of. Then, ' Thy Kingdom come '—my prayer for the Zenana Mission comes in there. Of course I knew all this before, but it all struck me with renewed force just then. We *do* need to learn unselfishness, forgetting our own precious selves. ' Looking unto Jesus.' "

The thought of Christian faith, and especially of Christian prayer, as a power that shrivels up the self-life was now constantly before Mary's mind. " You ask," she says in another letter, " how I pray. Well, the Lord's Prayer is my model. The disciples said ' Teach us to pray,' and Jesus gave them that. It can be expanded to any amount. And there is nothing selfish about it. Self does not come in till half-way through, and then it is not I, me, but ' give *us*,' ' lead *us*.' " Over in Edinburgh, about the same time, Henry Drummond was teaching the students that to be a Christian is to become *ec-centric*, to displace self and make Another the centre of all one's thought, feeling and action, remaining henceforth and for ever Christo-centric.

Mary felt in her youth " how hard it is," as Jesus candidly said, for the rich and prosperous, the healthy and happy to see the Kingdom of God and enter it. One evening she was sitting at the Windsor Church prayer meeting. " I was wondering," she says, " why Mr. Ferris and most ministers prayed so much for the sick, the dying, those in trouble and afflictions of all sorts, and never for those in prosperity, health, having all they could desire and yet in danger from that very prosperity. I felt left out in the cold."

But that evening her minister was inspired to give her just the message that she needed. "The Psalm was about idolatry, and I saw no particular interest in it for me; but in the next prayer Mr. Ferris applied it all to me, prayed for me, for all those who are tempted to put *anything* in the place of God. For I *am* in danger in that way, and the things that so engage my attention are not things that I could or should avoid. And yet I can trust God to keep me even from this danger."

Great as the perils of prosperity undoubtedly are, they need not daunt the spirit. The Rich Young Ruler can, if he will, enter the Kingdom of God, and have his happiness thereby increased a hundred-fold. Mary knew what it had cost her to enter the kingdom of music—seven years of strenuous toil. She remembered what Peter Arbo said about entering the kingdom of art—"all beautiful things are difficult." Could she refuse to pay the price of entering the Kingdom of God? She was too decided in character ever to do anything by halves. "Reason may understand a partial gift, a transient devotion; the heart knows only the entire sacrifice, and like the lover to the beloved, it says to its vanquisher, 'Thine alone and for ever.' "*

Instead of putting anything in the place of Christ, Mary resolved to give Him her life, her labour, her all. Not, however, by renouncing His fair world or avoiding her plain duties in it. Her bosom friend Emma Thomas was for a time attracted by the idea

* Sabatier's *Life of St. Francis*, p. 73.

of becoming a Sister of Charity, in the hope of ending
all perplexities by just being "told what to do."
Mary succeeded in dissuading her.   There was a
more excellent way—not to abjure the world and its
teeming interests, but to carry the blessings of the
Kingdom of God into it, and especially to face the
tremendous problem of lightening the darkness of its
age-long heathenism.

Mary's time of probation was now near an end.
Sometimes it had seemed long, but she saw it had
all been needed.   Especially she still felt that she
was lacking in courage, which she knew to be almost
synonymous with faith.   In June 1889 she wrote :
" For a long time I have been wishing I might have
some regular work, and it never yet seems to have
been God's will to give it me.   If that is so, I am
content not to have it, but to wait His time.   He is
teaching me always more and more, so patiently and
so gently, how I may trust everything to Him.   In
the meantime I must learn as much as I can—for one
thing, to be courageous.   Have you noticed how often
Paul asks his readers to pray for him that he may be
bold?   That, I have thought, is for me.   And I do
believe He can teach me this as well as other things I
thought nearly impossible."

Even a year later, in July 1890, we find her writing,
still in a mood of self-reproach, " I am no soldier."
It is an unusual confession for a woman of three-and-
twenty to make.   Most people would have said to her,
" Well, you needn't trouble very much about that.
Why not leave soldiering to the men? "   But she

evidently had other ideas. The great word " soldier " indicates her dream, her ambition, yes, her prayer, and she would never be satisfied until, as a good soldier of Jesus Christ, she was wearing the whole armour of God and using the weapons of the Spirit for the triumph of the Lord's Kingdom in the world.

Among those who first noted Mary's missionary zeal were her own minister, the Rev. James C. Ferris, of Windsor Church, and the Rev. (now Dr.) William Park, of Rosemary Street. She owed much to the teaching and friendship of both these men. Behind Mr. Ferris' retiring disposition there lay a geniality, sympathy and sense of humour which made him one of the most beloved of pastors and dearest of friends. He was born again in the Revival of 1859, the year in which Christ, entreated to come to Ireland, came in a rushing mighty wind and with tongues of living flame. The fire which kindled his youthful desire to be an evangelist continued to burn with steady glow all through his ministry, and his spiritual fervour was accompanied by a missionary passion, the evidences of which were apparent in the fact that both his Churches, First Newry and Windsor stood—as they still stand—in the front rank for missionary zeal and liberality. The other trait by which he is best remembered was his power of making the unseen and heavenly life real. Death was in his view always a going to the Father, and when his work was ending long before the evening hour of life, he quietly said, " If God wants me for the higher service, I am ready to go."

Mr. Park gave Mary wise counsel in critical days, and it was through him that God's clear call at length came to her. When she first writes of this eminent preacher to her Parisian friend Hélène, she depicts him as he was over thirty years ago, and the portrait is a speaking likeness still. "Next Monday," she begins, "Mr. Park is to give a lecture on 'Courtship and Marriage,' and he will do it well, I am sure, making it at once amusing and serious. He is the only one to choose a subject like that. He is, indeed, an astonishing man (*un homme étonnant*). His parish is one of the largest in Belfast, and he is a most exemplary Pastor, visiting his people often and forgetting none, holding meetings of every description, preaching twice every Sunday and conducting a Bible Class for the young, while on Thursday he has one for young ladies. Last Thursday I was present at this, and over a hundred were there. It is the International Lesson that he takes up, chiefly, I think, for the benefit of the teachers. And how well it is done; I would that you could hear him. With all that he is Director of Missions. It baffles me to understand how he can do it all."

Not very long afterwards Mary gave Hélène a great surprise. "I wonder," she writes, "if you imagine with what respect you ought at present to regard your friend. Do you know that I am now an Editor? Yes, and if this interests you, I am going to post to you, with this letter, a copy of my Magazine which has just appeared. It comes out only four times a year, so that it is no very great affair, but all the same it makes me think and enquire. It is the organ of our Ladies' Society for Missions in India (Gujarat) and China. The secretary of the Society sends me all the letters she receives from lady missionaries, and I extract from them the passages which I think interesting for the Magazine, and then I have to find other articles, to add notices of events bearing on the Society, and so forth. It is extremely interesting work, and I think all subscribers should be editors ! In that way they would interest themselves in the Mission and know something about it. I assure you that after reading and re-reading those articles I almost know them by heart."

How she was led to undertake the editorship of *Woman's Work* is best told by Dr. Park. "For many years," he says, "I had a Ladies' Class for an hour every Thursday afternoon, which was largely attended. Miss Crawford was one of the most regular members, and took a deep interest in the subjects that were discussed. At the time I happened to be the Convenor of the Foreign Mission, and had, among other duties, to prepare and issue the Quarterly Record of the Women's Association—popularly then known as the 'Pink Paper' from the colour of paper on which it was printed. Miss Crawford had such a well-cultivated mind, showed such thoughtfulness and wide information in her answers to questions, and was evidently filled with such missionary zeal that one day, after the class was over, I put before her the request that she should undertake the management of the Quarterly Paper. To this, after a little hesitation, she consented; and from that day onwards she gave a great part of her time and attention to it. The 'Pink Paper' soon developed, under her skill and loving care, into a regular magazine; and at last, from the excellence of its matter and the beauty of its illustrations, it attained a unique position (one might say, I think, without exaggeration) among all the women's missionary magazines of the world.''

It was in the spring of the Indian Mission Jubilee year (1890) that Mary was installed as editor of the missionary magazine. Later in the same year, after her grandfather's death, she seemed to hear another call, which moved her to the depths of her being. It was not, indeed, new to her, but it was louder, clearer and more insistent than ever before. She knew that there was urgent need for fresh workers in Gujarat, and it was '' in her heart '' to go. If Christ was beckoning her to the distant Mission Field, she would not be disobedient to the heavenly vision. After exchanging a few words with Mr. Park on the subject, she opened her heart to her parents. Writing to them from Mount Randal in September, when they were at the seaside, she said : '' This is by no means a new idea with me. For many years I have thought of it now and again, but I always thought that, being the only girl, if I could be of use at home it would not be right. But now the need seems so great, that perhaps it would be. right. Do not imagine that I like the idea of leaving home and friends, but I do think I love Christ better, and would like to serve Him as best I could. And I really think I would be happy.

. . . That day I met Mr. Park he did not say much, except that it was a matter we only could settle among ourselves. But he added, ' That would be grand.' "

Two months later Mr. and Mrs. Park were asked to come and talk the whole matter over at Mount Randal. " Of course," Mary wrote to her friend Ella, " Mr. Park would like me to go. He thinks it would be good for the Mission, perhaps making others think of the possibility of being spared from their homes. I assured him that it was many years since I had wanted to go. The fact is that I am not much more warm on that point now than I was two or more years ago, only I said nothing about it then. Mr. Park said this might show it was God's call. Then of course the matter of health was discussed, and Mr. Park's summing up of the whole thing was that the deciding seemed to rest with the doctor. As a first step towards getting medical advice, our doctor in Paris has been written to, and we are expecting his answer one of these days."

Dr. Louis Monod wrote as one who had been the friend as well as the physician of the Crawford family in Paris. His verdict regarding Mary's proposal was decisive. After recalling and describing " the grave malady of which she had long carried the germ," he says : " Placing myself at a purely medical point of view, I am absolutely opposed to her establishing herself either in Manchuria or in the province of Gujarat. If she were to go, she would, in my opinion, sacrifice her health, perhaps her life." Then he ventures to suggest that if she cannot become a foreign missionary she may be a home one. " Are there not in Ireland, in Belfast, around her, sorrowful ones to console, fallen to raise, heathen to convert? " And he concludes : " I have told you my thought, dear Monsieur Crawford, and I hope that, by the help of God, your daughter will, in the circumstances, be able to harmonise her affection for you with her zeal for the service of her Saviour."

It was clearly impossible to act against the advice of an expert, and a week later Mary wrote to her friend Ella : " I am not going to India or China. I could not help being disappointed when I heard the doctor's opinion. But it is right so, I am sure, and my prayers are answered. I asked that the way might be so plain that I would have no doubt, and so it is. Dr. Monod wrote a most kind and good letter; he is a real Christian man. He said a severe climate would be sure to bring back the weakness of my health and probably take my life. Of course there is but one way to decide."

At the same time it was neither her recognition of home duties nor her sympathy with the home heathen that kept her from the Mission Field. She made her point of view clear in a striking letter to Hélène. "If it had been a question of my marrying in order to go to a distant country, would you have said that it was my duty to remain with my parents? And I think my idea was much more profitable (*utile*) than that would have been. I have reflected a great deal for years past about my duty to others, and I saw that in the country of Gujarat, which is twice as large as Ireland, there are only six or seven lady missionaries. What can they do? And then I think that almost all girls regard themselves as useful and indispensable at home. And ought one to offer God only that which costs one nothing? I felt that I could not call myself indispensable at home so long as I had not spoken to my parents about it. That was not an easy thing to do. But now I see my duty clearly—always for the moment. And I know that it is where the will of God keeps me that I can best serve Him."

It was thus overruled that Mary was not to fulfil her missionary ideals by going to the Mission Field. She was never to see the land where both her grandfathers had preached the Gospel, and where her mother had first learned to lisp the Saviour's name. But if one door was closed to her, another, " great and effectual," stood wide open, and there she entered. If she was not permitted to be a missionary in the literal sense of the term, no one had a clearer call than she to be the friend of missionaries, the advocate of missions by pen and voice, and the teacher of little children among whom are the missionaries of the future. " She was a striking example," as Dr. Park writes, " of the fact that one who is hindered in the providence of God from becoming a foreign missionary —which she earnestly desired to be—may do as fine a work for the women of India and China as any missionary on the foreign field." To be entrusted with the double task of warming the Church's heart toward all the soldier-saints who were jeopardising

G

their lives on the high places of the field, and of
keeping the loneliest workers at the furthest out-
posts in affectionate relations with their sisters at the
home base, was to have a lifework which called forth,
as nothing else could have done, the best for the
highest.

It was easier at the beginning, and perhaps it
always remained more natural, for Mary to write than
to speak of the theme that lay nearest her heart.
" The gift of speaking," she confesses in an early
letter, " is not one of the gifts which God has given
me." But true as that might appear at the time,
she could not remain silent when once she realised
that she had not only a cause to plead but a Master
to honour. And ere long she proved that she was by
no means so tongue-tied as she had seemed. Always
admiring courage and devotion in others, she let her
own shy and timid nature be nerved by the strength of
faith, her reserve melted in the glow of a selfless
passion, until she became not only an invariably
effective but often a deeply moving speaker.

On the vexed question of the Ministry of Women
she apparently never had any difficulties, her intuitions
guiding her aright from the first. An interesting letter
shows that she and one of her dearest friends, who
"affected to disapprove of women speaking in public,"
had " little battles on that point," and " agreed to
differ on it." Then Mary chanced to hear that her
friend had for once been induced to speak at a Mothers'
Meeting. " I shall crow over her now," is her delighted

comment. Evidently she felt that her friend might yet go far enough, for what difference is there in principle between talking to a little group of mothers and moving a vast audience, as many a Zenana worker does, in the Assembly Hall?

Mary naturally began by addressing children. If she could speak to one Class, why not to a whole School? About the time when the question of her going or not going to India was hanging in the balance, she sent her friend Hélène a report of such an event. " What do you think—last Monday I addressed about sixty children of our Windsor Sunday School on Gujarat and our Mission there. You will ask how I had the courage to undertake such a thing, especially as several gentlemen were present conducting the meeting and showing Indian views with a magic lantern. I was surprised enough to see myself there in a room quite full. One of the teachers had asked me if I would *read* something, and almost before I knew what I was saying I told him I would like to *speak* something. I enjoyed doing it, but all the same it gave me much fatigue, for I could not sleep the night before or the night after. See what I get when I appear in public ! "

It was more difficult for her to face adults, as the following letter, written in October, 1892, clearly shows : " I think I told you how Marion Steen* wanted to get up a drawing-room meeting of young ladies and get *me,* if you please, to set the claims of Foreign

* Daughter of Dr. Robert Steen, of the Royal Belfast Academical Institution. Regarding her sister Annie see p. 219.

Mission work before them. I thought much about it, and came to the conclusion I really could not do it. Ever since, the idea has occasionally haunted me that perhaps I was unfaithful, disobedient to Christ, and not trusting enough in what He could do with a weak instrument. Marion's idea was to have some *young* person to speak. Will you ask that God will guide all this rightly, just as it will be most for His glory? I know Marion has not given up her idea, as she mentioned it to me one day of late."

What came of Miss Steen's proposal does not appear, but a year later we find Mary still chiding herself for her slowness to open her lips and plead the great cause of Foreign Missions. She had put Marion off by saying she had " counted the cost of being a missionary abroad but not of addressing meetings at home." Could that be her final answer? Having volunteered for the harder service, would she shrink back from the easier? One of her letters shows that her mind was troubled. " What sort of a servant of Jesus Christ am I? A miserably poor one, indeed. When the opportunity comes of speaking for Christ, the words often just depart from me, and I am dumb. I feel like hiding my head for shame. He is so good to me, I am often just overwhelmed by His goodness; how little it would be if I in turn would just speak for Him ! . . . He has taught me some things, and I know He will finish what He has begun." In her copy of one of Dr. Smellie's books these words are marked : " When the spirit lights up the Word for us, when He makes the love of

Christ the sweetest and surest thing in our world, when He pours His Own life into our nerves and souls, we simply cannot retain them to ourselves. The filling is followed by the overflow."

The following note to a friend shows that she did again " count the cost," drawing now upon resources which she had formerly overlooked. " When you think of me going to Raffrey to-morrow, lift up your heart in prayer to God that I may not try to speak there in my own strength, which is nothing but weakness, but that I may trust the Holy Spirit for the right words." And her next letter proves that the needed help was given. " I believe that my ordeal passed over all right. I was not frightened, and never realised until I was fairly started that I was preaching to the minister among others. The offering was very satisfactory."

The inspiring sense of being the channel of a power not her own was to accompany her through all the rest of her life. She was not always equally conscious of it, either in writing or in speaking. But the conviction of its reality always came back to her, and she felt it to be the one thing needful for effective service. " I have been thinking much," she writes in a letter, " about the Holy Spirit, waiting for and expecting His presence in work and life, and I find out how ' joy ' and ' the Holy Ghost ' go together. Whenever I lose that sense, it is through lack of prayer and reading in the right spirit. I think it is a splendid idea, *fact* I should rather say, that it is not on our own responsibility we go about God's work.   So often have I spoken because I thought I was in duty bound, and it went wrong. I like to remember how often Jesus said, ' The words that I speak, I speak not of myself, but my Father that dwelleth in Me, He doeth the works '; and with that, ' As Thou has sent me into the world, even so have I sent them into the world.' We are sent on the same understanding—we are not the responsible persons about the work."

Mary thus came to have the thrilling sense, at once so humbling and uplifting, of God's working *through* her. Regarding an article on " Prayer for Missions," which she wrote for *Woman's Work* (October, 1892), she says to a friend : " Do you know I have a very queer feeling about that little article. I feel as if it was not I who had written it. The main part of it floated through my mind for months, but at the thought of putting it on paper my heart always sank. I couldn't. I had no words. Then suddenly one evening two or three weeks ago, as I quietly sat in my room, the words came crowding into my mind. I quickly took pencil and note-book and scribbled away as hard as I could, though it was late. You know, to write fast is quite against my usual habit. Then I went to bed thankful. Of course, afterwards it took several hours to put it into proper shape. . . . I don't want ever to write anything unless I am sure it is God's teaching. It would be dreadful to *make up* pious words. I often feel that strongly in reference to my Sunday School Class. I hope it is not egotistical for me to write this to you. I thought it would interest you, and it is one of God's loving-kindnesses to me."

Her love for the Kingdom of Christ among the heathen now burned with a steady flame. After listening to a drawing-room address by Amy Carmichael, one of her warmest Belfast friends, she writes : " Amy is quite absorbed with the idea of the great need of the heathen, and she succeeded in enthusing me very much. I wish I could put the enthusiasm into words." She rejoiced whenever she heard of any young women volunteering for Mission work. Such sentences as the following occur frequently in her letters : " Amy's sister is in a Deaconess Institution preparing for the Foreign Field." "It comforts me to think of our good Medicals getting ready." " It makes me glad to remember the good workers that are being trained for us in Edinburgh."

The Foreign Missionaries of her Church became her joy and her crown. They were the channels of God's grace to His heathen children. Their labours were the modern Acts of the Apostles. As they were doing the work she had so desired to do, her sympathy with them had a tender personal element. And is not Christ's power perfected—" fully felt "—in human weakness? "When we workers," she wrote, "are so frail, it does show how the work is God's and not ours. ' We have this treasure in earthen vessels, that the excellency of the power may be of God and not of us.' It is wonderful that He can and does use us, when we are so weak."

Thus she could change the minor into the major key. And she could do so when it was not any fallible human workers of whom she was thinking, but the unerring Divine Worker. In November, 1892, she tells Hélène of a disaster which " cast a shadow over all the north of Ireland," the wreck of the *Roumania,* with two of the best Irish missionaries—Mrs. Beatty and Dr. Mary MacGeorge— on board. She feels—so she writes— that she ought to be wearing mourning for them, and it is hard not to ask, with Mr. Park, " Why does God permit the wind and waves to work such havoc? Why did He not put His hand over and shelter those who bravely and unselfishly, in answer to His call, were going forth to do His work in a heathen land? " Certainly, she reflects, His ways are not our ways. But she knows, and it is enough to know, that He does all things well. And the front page of the next *Woman's Work* sounded a clarion call by her Aunt Harriet, ending with the words :

Yet still the Lord Jehovah reigns,
    And He whose grace was strong in these
Can call from Erin's hills and plains
    A host to serve Him if He please;

Can make our mourning Zion rise
    With love new-kindled, sorrow-stirred,
Can bid her view with startled eyes
    The heathen waiting for the Word.

Mary loved all the missionaries who brought the spirit of the East, the breath of fresh mission fields, into the home Church. She knew that they were all workers before they were speakers, and that it was just their enthusiasm for Christ's cause in heathen lands that developed their gift of moving and melting speech. One or two instances must be given, as her final *apologia,* if such be needed, for Woman's Ministry. In June, 1905, she writes : " We have just had Mrs. Hunter (of Kwangning) for a week. We lived mostly out of doors. We had long talks on the Mission and spiritual matters. On Sunday she came to my class and talked about her women. The girls were delighted. She did not speak at the Annual Meeting, being too tired by all her meetings through the winter. She had a letter from her husband saying how much work is ready to her hand when she goes out in September. She said if she had had that letter before the Assembly, she could not have helped speaking."

These last words go to the root of the matter. " She could not have helped speaking." The undeniable truth is, that when woman's heart is full to overflowing, she is moved no less than man to " prophesy "—as Philip's daughters did—and that the Divine Spirit equally aids her. " We cannot but speak the things we have seen and heard." When the human spirit is under a constraint like that, "there is no longer male or female." One other instance will suffice. " Mrs. O'Neill (of Fakumen) is with us. She has been having a lot of meetings, and is a capital speaker, like her husband. They are full of enthusiasm for their work." What need to labour the point? To be enthusiastically silent is impossible! "The Lord gave the word: the women that publish the tidings are a great host."

Justly proud, however, as Mary was of the missionary army, and especially of the Irish division of it, she saw it as a tiny band in comparison with the host of volunteers who will spring to life in the day of the Lord's power. She always felt in her heart the ache of an unrealised ideal. One wonders how many mothers all over the Church received from her little notes like the following: "If at any time your daughter is passing this way and could stop here for a night or two to visit me, I should be very pleased. I know of her desire to be a missionary, and I like to get to know such." Girls halting between two opinions, allured by dreams of social success and yet sighing for something better, learned in happy talks with her that all the splendid gifts of culture, beauty and wealth attain their crowning glory only when they are consecrated to Christ and His Kingdom. She was doubtless a good organiser, but that was the last word one thought of applying to her. In her eyes the Church was not an organisation. It was the Body of Christ. And because "we are members one of another," she sought to establish personal relations with all her fellow-workers, especially with those who were, or who might one day be, Christ's servants sent far hence unto the Gentiles.

Mary knew well what was being done by all the Churches of the world on behalf of Foreign Missions, and there was one that stirred her admiration above all the rest. " One Church," she wrote, " puts us all to shame. It is small, and few of its members are wealthy, most are poor; yet out of their poverty they give much. It is a usual, instead of an unusual, thing for its members to place themselves unreservedly in Christ's hands, to work for Him at home or abroad, as He thinks fit. So while one in every 1,770 of *our* professing Christians goes abroad, one in 66 of the Moravian Church is working to spread the Gospel in the ' regions beyond.' Surely the *profession* of the Moravians must oftener be real than among ourselves. Have we not reason to humble ourselves and to arise and really *do* the work we have only as yet begun? "

Mary occasionally attended Christian Conventions, and liked them in proportion as the speakers were filled with zeal for Foreign Missions and sought to communicate their enthusiasm to their hearers. In the summer of 1892 she and her cousin Ina Huston (now Mrs. Hamilton Martin) went to such a gathering at Fenaghy. " Mr. Park," she reports, " gave a first-rate opening address in the Foreign Missions tent, full of things to be remembered " (and reproduced in *Woman's Work,* Oct. 1892). From this tent she went to a meeting "for the deepening of spiritual life," but " did not find it very profitable, though one or two of the speeches were good. I think some of these people looked too much to man to deepen their spiritual life, whereas I think this work belongs entirely to God, and when once people know Him, He teaches each of them in a different way." And in the end she says, " I don't think I would go to Fenaghy again unless I thought I could do some good.   I think that in religion as in other things we must beware of selfishness—always getting and giving little. I feel the sort of getting I need more than anything is that which comes through prayer and communion with God. On the whole I think the Foreign Missions meeting might have been called ' for the deepening of spiritual life,' because I do think hearty work for Foreign Missions does just that better than many things. Of course any kind of hearty work for Christ does it. But this is such a great and necessary work."

Later in the same year, when Mr. D. L. Moody was moving all Ireland, Catholics in the South and West as well as Protestants in the North flocking to hear him, Mary's first thought was, " We must pray that the result may be a great victory for the Kingdom of Christ in Ireland. I am sure it will result in a great stirring of the Christian people to renewed activity."   And her second thought was, " Surely, too, all this will stir up a far greater concern for the heathen. Do you notice that both for the Foreign Missions and Zenana several workers are wanted just now? It is a pity that money should now be lying unused because we have no volunteers to send.   I wonder if we wouldn't have all the workers we need if we prayed for them."

Devoted workers, actual and potential, were her heart's desire. It used to be said that " many religious women are more religious than moral, more emotional than practically helpful in every-day life."[*]

[*] Dr. Whyte, *Samuel Rutherford*, p. 41.

But that is rapidly becoming a thing of the past. The typical woman of to-day dreads nothing so much as an emotional piety that ends in itself. Mary never lost the opportunity of attending any important Missionary Conference—the most memorable were those of Liverpool (1896) and Edinburgh (1910)—but she never went to Keswick. To a friend who urged her to go she answered : " I don't agree with you. I have no desire (at present) to go. I have a feeling that I can hardly assimilate and work out all the good teaching I already get, and that it would only have a hardening effect to get more. Do you understand? " No doubt if she had gone she would have found many ardent friends of Missions. But to the end she remained sensitively alive to what she regarded as the Convention danger—of absorbing without diffusing, of aspiring to be a saint without becoming a soldier, of pursuing holiness and even perfection as if they were separable from the enthusiasm of humanity, of seeking to have the Kingdom of God inwardly, without working and fighting incessantly for its triumph in the whole great world which God loves and for which Christ died.

The finest of all missionary literature, Mary discovered early, is the Epistles of St. Paul, and the best preparation for understanding them is that baptism of the missionary spirit which is the modern Pentecost. The desire to see all lands penetrated with the light of the Gospel unites minds far apart in time and space. Lovers of Missions see eye to eye across the ages. " All the spare time I have just now," Mary wrote about the end of 1892, " I am giving to reading Conybeare and Howson's *Life and Epistles of Paul.* It is a wonderfully entrancing book to me. It is delightful reading the Epistles as they occur in Paul's history. The original translations given in the book throw much light on them. I feel that I am living with Paul, getting to know him as a real person. I am sure this will be a help with teaching. I shall feel that I have a grasp of the subject, more, at least, than I had."

In such company she could never regret her resolve to devote her life to the cause of Foreign Missions. That is saying too little. All the best workers for God and His Kingdom have been regarded by enemies, and sometimes even by friends, as more or less crazy. Mary did not quite escape that reproach. After paying a series of visits in the autumn of 1907, she writes : " On thinking these visits over, they seem all in some way connected with the Zenana Mission ! Miss X., I think, considers me rather cracked on that subject. The home slum dwellers appeal to her more. But you know how I was called to that work, and there seem so few for it compared to the thousands who are trying to help the home heathen." And in quiet self-defence she adds : " We don't neglect the home ones. Many people consider that my father gives much more for Foreign than for Home. He told me lately that he was counting up his givings for ten years back, and found that the proportion was 27 per cent. Foreign and 73 per cent. Home." At the same time she came to recognise that the modern distinction of Home and

Foreign, like the ancient cleavages between Jew and Gentile, Greek and Barbarian, is profoundly misleading. The Divine Founder of Missions allowed no such differences. For Him there is but one field, white unto harvest. Two watchwords, representing Home and Foreign, were therefore always united in Mary's thoughts—" Ireland for Christ " and " The world for Christ." Each of them is the opposite of " ourselves alone."

About the time of the Edinburgh Missionary Conference, Mary asked the readers of *Woman's Work* (July, 1910), to use " the Lord's Prayer as a Missionary Prayer." And was she not essentially right? Even the expansion of the central petition for daily bread is not inappropriate, and the whole missionary interpretation became so dear to her that it must find a place here. " *Our Father which art in Heaven,* looking down on all Thy children throughout the world; *Hallowed be Thy Name,* Thine alone, and not the names of gods of wood and stone; *Thy Kingdom come,* in all hearts, and in all heathen lands; *Thy will be done,* by us who have learned that Thy will is the spread of the everlasting Gospel; *Give us this day our Daily Bread,* and give us grace to share the Bread of Life with those who have it not; *Forgive us our trespasses,* our selfishness in closing our eyes to the heathen world's need of Christ; *And lead us not into temptation,* the temptation of self-pleasing, luxury, and forgetfulness of Thy cause; *But deliver us from evil,* by giving us larger-heartedness and wider sympathies; *For Thine is the Kingdom,* which one day will come; *and the Power* to use in Thy work even such weak instruments as we; *and the Glory,* for without Thee we can do nothing; *for ever and ever. Amen."*

One can imagine with what feelings Mary listened to the words addressed by the Archbishop of Canterbury to his " Fellow-workers in the Church Militant " at the opening of that great Edinburgh Conference. " Be quite sure that the place of Missions in the life of the Church must be the central place, and none other. That is what matters. Let people get hold of that, and it will tell—it is the merest commonplace to say so—it will tell for us at home as it will tell for those afield. Secure for that thought its true place, in our plans, our policy, our prayers, and then—why, then, the issue is His, not ours. But it may well be that, if that come true, ' there be some standing here who shall not taste of death till they see ' here on earth, in a way we know not now, ' the Kingdom of God come with power.' "

Seven years later, in the tumult of the world war, Mary found her heart's great desire equally well expressed (see *Woman's Work,* January, 1918) by a soldier lying in hospital, with shrapnel wounds which refused to heal, and just waiting. " Strange, isn't it," he said, " that my thoughts always go back to the one theme of Foreign Missions. Why does our Church keep Foreign Missions so much in the background? Something is wrong with the scheme of things which fails to put *the whole world for Christ* in the foreground as the battle cry of the Christian

Church.   My little money will presently be found
devoted to the cause.   But what is that?   We can
carry nothing out whither I go.   My message is that
all those who are wise should work in the service
while it is day, remembering the coming night."

The end is Christ's victory everywhere, and the
means, His sacrifice and ours.   As Mary heard the late
Professor Denney say: " There must be a passion in
the answer of the soul to Christ that answers to the
passion of His love to us, and there must be emphasis
laid on Christ's demand for renunciation.   Christ asks
for men and women to give themselves to Him, and
not to an easy service, but to something the symbol of
which is the Cross.   When Garibaldi summoned young
Italy he said : ' I do not offer pay, provisions or quar-
ters; I offer thirst, forced marches, battles, and death.'
It was to that cry that the deep heart of his people
responded, and when a voice like that is uttered by men
who have the right to utter it, then we can be sure that
the thin ranks will fill up again and our King go forth
conquering and to conquer.' "*

* " Addresses at World Missionary Conference," p. 328 f.

H

CHAPTER V

THE SANCTUARY OF HOME

EARLY in 1893 Miss Crawford became engaged
to Mr. Robert Brown, of Agharainy, in County
Tyrone. There was already a friendship between the
families, two of Mary's aunts having married
cousins of Mr. Brown. Mary had first met her
future lover at Newcastle, County Down, in the
holiday season of 1880, when he was nineteen and
she a schoolgirl of thirteen, and the climbing of Slieve
Donard together on a long summer day was an event
never forgotten, though half a dozen years make a
big difference to those who are still in their teens.
While she remained in Paris they saw little more of
each other, but after she came to live in Belfast they
met much oftener. Mr. Brown was not musical, but
music had not the highest place in her heart and life.
In the great things that make for human happiness
they were kindred spirits, and the Guiding Hand
united their lives. For five-and-twenty years she was
to be his helpmeet and comrade, the sharer of all his
hopes and aims, the good angel of his pilgrimage.

Cherishing the highest—in some sense the sacramental—ideal of marriage, in which there is ever " a sense of something holy, a shadow of something vast," Mary had not so much reasoned opinions as infallible intuitions regarding the obligation of Christians to marry only Christians. It was to her unthinkable that our Lord should ever lead any disciple of His to form a lifelong union of heart and soul with an enemy or even a stranger to Himself and His Kingdom. In any temptation to compromise she saw not so much a case of conscience to solve, as a question of personal loyalty to answer, a crucial test of Christian honour to undergo. On a theme so vitally related to her faith, two or three sentences from her letters, marked by even more than her ordinary directness and simplicity, will perhaps be permitted. " I am sure that God has given us to one another to help us to walk in His way. I should not be happy if I did not think so. I am so glad that it is by His leading that you and I have come to the place where we are. We are heirs together of the grace of life, and our prayers are not hindered, they are helped. Mine are ever so much. . . . Don't let us get so taken up with other things as to neglect our Best Friend. The temptation is often great with me, but I am never happy if there is coldness and distance between Him and me. It makes me glad to think that the Lord Jesus was my lover long before you, and I gave my heart to Him. I do not say that lightly." Again she writes : " On the subject of Nehemiah's reforms, Mr. Park had been speaking very seriously about

Christian young men marrying girls who make no profession of Christianity, and *vice versa*. He said he could not understand it, neither can I. With you and me it is ' in the Lord,' and it makes me glad to think of that." . . . Keenly alive to faults in herself to which other eyes might be blind, she says, " You will have to learn ' patience,' real, not a game." On the old and ever new problem of obedience she held sensible modern views of equal partnership. " I do not say I shall always do what *you* consider right, but I shall consider it seriously." And regarding another question in which every woman is interested—the secret of loveliness—her mysticism recalls an old charm, rarely believed, never advertised, but infallible. " I am quite content that you should think me beautiful, and for your sake I shall try to be so. If I grow in the knowledge of Christ it will be so." Is it not written of St. Brigid of Kildare, the greatest of Irishwomen, that " She was not only good, but she was beautiful. Sin is the ugliest thing in the world, and it generally happens that the more people try to become like Jesus, the more does His great beauty come into their faces."*

In later years Christian girls would sometimes seek Mary's advice when they were faced with the question of accepting or declining an offer of marriage. The purport of her answer was always the same : " See that you really love one another, and that you agree on things vital." To a friend in sore perplexity she wrote : " I am entirely at one with you as to the

* *Stories of the Irish Saints,* J. Sinclair Stevenson.

SHORTLY BEFORE HER MARRIAGE.

necessity of mutual affection and of sympathy on the question of religion. I cannot at all understand how intelligent persons with affectionate natures can be happy on any other terms. For me love and religion are indispensable. I should greatly like to see you married if these conditions were fulfilled, but meanwhile you do well to keep your mind fully occupied, for work is a real benediction, as I have often seen."

Mr. Park thought it likely that as a betrothed lover Mary would feel constrained to resign the editorship of *Woman's Work*. But there is no indication that the idea of so doing ever once occurred to her. She had become the *fiancée* of one who was convinced that woman no less than man should be free to follow her own ideals. And she was not long in setting Mr. Park's mind at rest. " I was at his class this afternoon," she wrote one day in March. " After it was over he came up to me and said, ' I fear I shall have to look out for a new Editor.' ' I hope not,' I answered. ' I hope not, too,' he said, and that was all."

That was all, but how much was involved in her decision ! By continuing all her editorial functions and missionary labours, she was not only to render a lifelong service to the whole Church she loved, but to refute the widely current though mistaken idea that strenuous official activities are in a woman incompatible with the discharge of private duties and the full enjoyment of domestic life. She might have coveted a quiet seclusion within the fence of a devout home-life, far removed from the anxiety and strain of public affairs, and few would have blamed her. But in that case her name would never have become dear in the mission fields of Asia, nor would any memoir of her ever have been required.

Soon after this Mary had a happy interview with Mr. Park at his manse. "He showed me," she says, "a lot of missionary papers which he gets, and advised me to get one or two more than I do, and lent me a variety of literature of various kinds which we talked about. Then he took me up to his study. I saw his wonderful desk, the fame of which had reached me. In one of the folding sides there are forty drawers, in the other as many pigeon holes. Every nook of space is utilised, and he has everything so tidy. He showed me a catalogue of all kinds of patent desk arrangements, and I greatly admired them." Probably she was beginning to feel the need of something of the same kind. At any rate, she had written to Hélène a little before in these terms : " My Magazine gives me a lot of correspondence, which is always increasing. I must become entirely business-like (*tout à fait une femme d'affaires*) in order to get through it all more quickly. I waste much time by losing papers and having afterwards to find them again. You know I am not naturally a very orderly person. But I must learn to be one."

There is ample evidence that she succeeded. Even in the time of her engagement she tried to allow nothing to interfere with her editorial duties. "I must," she writes, "give some quiet, undisturbed days to *Woman's Work,* when I can sit down for

several hours and think and plan. If I get a
few days when I can absorb myself completely in
it, that will do largely." Much of her
strength always lay just in her sense of weakness, in the
swiftness and sureness of her self-criticisms. " Last
time," she says, " I was not able to throw myself into
the work properly, and I know many points about it
which were in consequence weak. When I read in
other papers, such as *Regions Beyond,* things that
stir my heart, I feel sure they were prepared with
much prayer, and I know it is the sort of preparation
that will make our magazine of use." As she neared
the goal of her summer number, she had for once the
assistance of her friend Maude MacBride. " She
helped me," the editor writes, " to copy out the last
remains of material, and then we went down town to
leave the MS. with the printer. We were glad to be
together for a few days before the ' new chapter.' "
This next chapter was not to be literal but figurative;
written without pen and ink, it was to appear in
the " woman's work " of life.

Finding out the subtle differences which love made
in her life, Mary tried to share her sense of them
with her friend Hélène. " Everything is enhanced
(*tout est grandi*), joy, and responsibility, and also
sorrow." Nature revealed new meanings to her, and
something said by her *fiancé* in praise of the lovely
Mourne Mountains calls forth these reflections : " I am
so glad you love mountains, for I delight in them too.
I do think it lifts one's heart up to God to be among
them and see them in their beauty. I think an

occasional day among them as good as a sermon. Any time that God speaks to us directly is as good as His Word read; better, I think, than His Word spoken. It is well we have His two books. I like very much Psalm 19, which describes them both. The second of the two is better, though; from the first we could not know of Christ, and He said, ' No man cometh unto the Father but by me.' I fancy that the better we know the second book the better we shall be able to read the first."

Her lover, like herself, was interested in Sunday School work, and one of her letters indicates how she regarded a teacher's duties. " Do you ever feel just as you are going out that you very much wish you had another hour to give to preparation? I do. It is very often during the last hour that I have got my ideas straightened, and when the time comes for going out I would like time to go over everything again in my own mind. When the good ideas come I am always so thankful, and take it as a good gift from God, because I know that when His Spirit is not with me my mind is a blank, and I am quite unable to speak of Christ and His love. I find help for my teaching a very definite thing to pray for."

By this time Mary's strongly individual character was fully formed, and it had the peculiar charm which accompanies self-reverence, self-knowledge, self-control. If she had formerly been too prone, as she confesses, to imitate others, that time was long past, and she could now justify the instinct which bade her prove her loyalty to her one ideal by being true to herself. " I think I am learning more and more how God does not want us to be copies of one another, but only to look at our one Example, and then we shall all be different. It has always been a great source of discouragement to me to compare myself with others. Just about ten years ago (a great date for me) it was reading Miss Havergal that made me so miserable. I am finding how good it is that I have Jesus Christ to lean on. He takes such pains to teach each of us separately, and give us just the teaching we need. It is to Him alone we must look; we are not obliged to please a host of earthly teachers. That is so restful."

Few can realise how hard, as a rule, it is for a woman of artistic temperament to give her mind adequately to the theory and practice of housekeeping. If Mary was to succeed in doing all the duties enumerated in Proverbs xxxi, it could only be by the exercise of will. Excusing herself for not promising to write her *fiancé* daily, she offers this joco-serious explanation : " Papa says that when he was in your circumstances, he made twice a week do him. He had a whole year and a half or more of it to look forward to, and ruinous postage there was from Paris in those days. Willy,* however, reminds me that there are *two* posts in the day. But I presume you do not want me to unlearn all the good housekeeping I have for the past years been acquiring with such pains; so that is why I do not promise to write every day. I am really trying to be a very good housekeeper. It will take all the trying I am capable of to succeed in that."

* Her third brother who entered the Indian Civil Service.

If the Editor might hope to continue her work without a break, the Sunday School teacher could not. When the time for summer holidays came, Mary had her last Sunday with her pupils at Windsor. "Yesterday I said good-bye to my class," she wrote next day. " I was sorry, sorry to think it was my last opportunity of talking with my girls, but we had a nice day to finish up with. I love those girls, and if they have learned half as much as I have during all these years I have been with them, it is well."

One of the pupils, herself now a teacher in Windsor, speaks for many. " My sister and I were in Miss Crawford's class, and no one who had that privilege can ever forget her teaching. As small girls we didn't at first realise how fortunate we were, but ere long we awoke to the fact that we had a very exceptional teacher, though perhaps it was only when we became teachers ourselves that we understood how much hard work must have gone to the preparation of each week's lesson. Not long ago she made the remark to me, ' You know, I really *love* teaching.' . . . She never preached at us, but tried to get at our ideas, and encouraged us to discuss the lesson as much as possible. What I remember most vividly is the quiet, methodical way the work was done; there was no apparent effort to gain our attention, no striving after effect, yet our interest seldom wavered, and the lessons taught were not forgotten. . . . I don't remember hearing her utter one word of reproof; if an ' unruly member ' talked to her neighbour or let her attention wander for a moment, a

gentle hand was laid on her knee while the lesson
went on uninterrupted, and that was quite enough—
her very gentleness made us well-behaved. Our class
was one of the largest in the school, and the members,
as in most city schools, were constantly changing, but
she took a personal interest in every one of the girls,
and that interest did not cease with their membership,
but followed them through years. I don't suppose
there is one of those girls who does not feel her
influence to the present."

The severing of home ties is always the hardest of
partings. " I was quite touched," Mary writes, " when
one of our maids burst into tears. I had no idea they
would mind. I do hope that not many people will
weep, though; it would be too trying. If my parents
did so, I think I should be torn in pieces." Finally
she writes : " This is the last Sunday we shall be
together as of old. The end of this chapter cannot but
be a bit sad. I should not certainly wish it to be otherwise either. I should not like to be only glad at
leaving my old home. All these thoughts were pretty
persistent this morning, but there was a great deal of
comfort in the words Mr. Ferris read in Deut. xxxiii.
There are some wonderful things there. All the
blessings begin with the love that our God has
for His people, and end up with the happiness of the
people that belong to Him."

On August the 16th the marriage ceremony was per-
formed by Mr. Ferris and Dr. Watts, in the presence of
friends who filled Windsor Church. A month later Mrs.
Brown wrote to Hélène a letter in which the Rhine,

Lucerne, St. Beatenberg, Mürren, and Grindelwald are prominent. Her wonder was fresh as a happy child's. " I had no idea that there was in the world a country so magnificent as Switzerland. Lucerne and the sails on all parts of the beautiful lake are delicious. We went up the Rigi (by train!) and had the good fortune to witness a perfect sunrise. It was wonderful to see the absolute clearness of the atmosphere at five o'clock, whereas we were told that on the two preceding mornings the mountains had been almost completely hidden." They came back by London, where they met Mr. and Mrs. Crawford returning from a trip in Devonshire, and all four spent a couple of days making purchases for Agharainy, which was to be Mary's home for the rest of her life.

This abode of ancient peace is situated in the parish of Donaghmore, towards the south of County Tyrone, where one is always reminded of the words of one of the metrical Psalms—

> The little hills on every side
> Rejoice right pleasantly.

The village of Donaghmore, with its fine old Irish Cross, is about three miles west of the old town of Dungannon, with which it is connected by a straight highway and delightfully crooked byways. The house of Agharainy was purchased by Mr. James Brown, Robert's father, from a gentleman who held a lease of the farm at the peppercorn rental of fourpence an

AGHARAINY, DONAGHMORE.

THE CHILDREN'S HOUSE

acre, until friends advised him to build himself a good house. When he had done so, he found it necessary, in true Hibernian fashion, to sell the land in order to pay for the house, after which he went to America to retrieve his fortunes. From time to time extended and modernised, the house is now all ivy-mantled.

Set in the midst of old trees, gardens, and orchards, with deep meadows and thick hedgerows beyond, it is a very attractive dwelling-place, in which Mary was from the very first perfectly at home. Though born in one city and bred in another, she could never quite reconcile herself to town life, while she always loved the simple joys of the country. Between her spirit and Agharainy there was therefore a pre-established harmony, and during all the five-and-twenty years in which she was " the angel of the house," it was never long without guests—beloved kinsfolk and friends, missionaries welcomed as King's messengers, or tired and lonely city workers, all of whom found refreshment for body and soul in breathing the air of that quiet resting-place. As Miss Helen Waddell writes : " That house was really the ' House Beautiful,' built by the Lord of the Hill for the relief and security of pilgrims. Missionaries went there before going out; most of them, certainly if they were distressed in mind, body, or estate, came there for long leisurely breathing-spaces when they were home on furlough."

Nature does many wonderful things, and doubtless had no small share in the making of such a home. But something diviner than the beauty and repose of Nature was needed, and its presence is indicated in words like these : " Every morning I pray definitely for the Holy Spirit for each member of the household—for the sweetening of our ordinary life, our ordinary communications one with the other. And that is certainly given. A peaceful, loving spirit pervades all."

Agharainy was ere long musical with the voices of children—first, two boys, Laurence and Oliver, then two girls, Alice and Honor, and lastly another boy, Alan. Each of them was to the mother a wonder-child, coming, as one of her favourite writers says, " out of the everywhere into here," suggesting strange riddles about eyes and ears, hands and feet, smiles and tears.

How did they all just come to be you?
God thought about me, and so I grew.

But how did you come to us, you dear?
God thought about you, and so I am here.

Mrs. Brown—who always remained " Mary " to her wide circle of friends—wrote thus to another young mother : " Judging by my experience, there is no greater joy than comes with a dear child of your very own. And as he grows the joy and comfort also grow." From this time onward her letters are full of the mother-love which is woman's purest earthly happiness, unless it be excelled by that joy in the Lord's service which had already dwelt long in the same passionate heart, the joy which inspired the young Galilean mother who said :

> My soul doth magnify the Lord,
> And my spirit rejoices in God my Saviour.

Mary's eldest brother Alexander had by this time offered himself for the Mission Field, just as she had done, and in his case the doctors put no barrier in the way. Completing his studies in the spring of 1895, he was ready to start for China. To all the family his going was a source of mingled sorrow and pride. "Alek's ordination," Mary writes, "is to be in the beginning of April, and we want to be there. Papa intends going to America with him. The China letters urge Alek's coming out immediately. As the French say, ' Cela m'a serré le cœur ' (that wrung my heart), when I realised that the dear boy might really be away so soon. How many years it may be till we see him again ! But it is splendid to think how useful he may be. One day he said to me, ' People speak of the danger in going to China; even looking at Mr. Wylie's and Dr. Greig's experiences I am not afraid. It is not death I fear; life seems more to be afraid of.' He means the responsibility of living well." . . . Later she writes : " The parting was trying, and yet how glad we are at his errand. As Martha, my R.C. maid, says, ' He has gone on a good mission.' An old neighbour of the same persuasion, when I said I had been to Belfast for my brother's ordination, said so fervently, ' Thank God for that.' So indeed we do thank God. I think it will be so good telling Laurence about Uncle Alek away in China. It will be a practical lesson in Christian usefulness. I have a good-sized map of Manchuria which I intend to keep in a prominent place."

In the same spring Mary conceived a surprising idea, of which she writes the following note : " I am making a weekly pilgrimage to Belfast now. We have lately had an excursion day instituted, and I am taking singing lessons ! Doesn't it seem rather perverse to have them now when so much travelling is involved and not when I was within easy reach? But you see I did not and *do not* intend to set up as a singer, but I must sing to my dear ones at home, especially on Sundays, for they always wish it, and I don't like doing it in such a very middling way. I don't want this talked about much, for I am a *pianist,* not a singer. This gives me nearly four hours in the train every week."

Such an unobtrusive act is too characteristic of her to be passed unnoticed. If *playing* counted as her five talents, which she made into ten, *singing* was her one talent, which she would not bury in the earth ! Overcoming the natural tendency to despise a minor gift, she cultivated it with all due care, finding reward enough in giving pleasure within the circle of her own home, where " love can make a little gift excel." Is it not true that the best portion of a good life consists in " little, nameless, unremembered acts of kindness and of love "? The spirit that prompts them is never forgotten.

In the summer of the same year (1895) Mary's Norwegian school friend, Emma Thomas, who had lost first her brother Edwin and then her mother, came to Ireland to be comforted. During her stay at Agharainy she made very interesting jottings in her diary, of which two or three may be given. "Saturday, June 29 : We spoke of the future life and of the occupations which will then be assigned to us. Mary told me of her grandfather (Dr. Glasgow), who loved to talk of that subject, and of the Heaven whither his thoughts often tended. . . . Sunday, July 7 : This dear friend has something translucid or transparent in the look which prayer and intimate communion with God give her. She chose at the end of the day the 116th Psalm, which she believes the Lord chose on His last evening with His disciples before He went to the Garden. . . . Sunday, July 14th : Walk with Mary. We always talk so well together, and she does me so much good. Prayer alone, she said, is not always sufficient, and we do not have recourse enough to the Word—to the reading of the Bible, which is the daily bread our soul requires. . . . Tuesday, July 16 : We talked of the past and our beloved dead. She has the full conviction that they can follow us and aid us in that which leads to good, as the Apostle says in the 11th chapter of Hebrews."

All things considered, Mary's life was as full in the quiet of the country as it had been in the bustle of Paris or Belfast. The books and papers which claimed her first attention had always a direct bearing upon *Woman's Work*, but her letters show that she

I

found time for a good deal of other reading. She is charmed with Ruskin's *Ethics of the Dust* and George Macdonald's *Alec Forbes;* she pronounces the Life of Henry Drummond excellent; and she finds *Isabel Carnaby* amusing and nice and good. She quotes a reviewer who says that " in a novel one should look for mental and moral beauty," and adds " quite my sentiments." The following note on a great book of another class is interesting : " When in Belfast I got, as I thought, Dr. G. A. Smith's *Isaiah,* but find they handed me by mistake the second volume of the *Minor Prophets.* I think I shall change it. This volume seems fuller of criticism than the first, and he says he has not so much space for the practical applications, which are the part I like. Laurence, looking over my shoulder, says : ' What is C for? ' I say ' Criticism.' He asks, ' What is Criticism? ' Too hard for an infant." . . . In the next letter she writes : " I have finished the first volume of *Isaiah* and don't intend to read more till I re-read and try to digest. It is splendid."

Mary's sense of all the happiness she owed to her Christian faith came vividly home to her in reading of Mrs. Carlyle and Mrs. Browning, in the one case with a perplexing feeling of contrast, in the other with a delightful consciousness of spiritual affinity. " Mama," she says, " has been reading *Mrs. Carlyle* to me, a book I have long been anxious to know. I is wonderfully interesting. She was a strange woman, so clever and lively and amusing, very kind to her old servants, etc., but without religion. The reading of such a Life gives me such a cold, dreary feeling. It is very sad near the end, when she cannot help crying, ' Will God hear me, who have constantly neglected Him all my life? ' "

In Mrs. Browning's letters, on the other hand, Mary found just what her spirit craved, and for an invalid friend of her own she transcribes this arresting passage : " To Miss Mitford, a dear friend very ill.—Pray for you? I do not wait that you should bid me. May the divine love in the face of our Lord Jesus Christ shine upon you day and night, and make all our human love strike you as dull and cold in comparison with that ineffable tenderness ! As to wandering prayers, I cannot believe it is of conse- quence whether this poor breath of ours wanders or does not wander. If we have strength to throw our- selves upon Him for everything, for prayers as well as for the ends of prayer, it is enough and He will prove it to be enough presently. I have seen when I could not pray at all. And then God's face seemed so close upon me there was no need of prayer, any more than if I were near *you* as I yearn to be, as I ought to be, there would be need for this letter."

In the beginning of 1896 Mr. and Mrs. Brown went to Liverpool to attend the Student Volunteer Inter- national Missionary Conference. She sent her first vivid impressions to her friend Miss Martin, and after- wards wrote a fuller account for *Woman's Work*. In her letter she says : " I don't know when I was at anything I enjoyed so much, and Robert no less. It seemed to me like the Jews travelling in parties up to

Jerusalem to devote some days entirely to worshipping God. I felt like that. Dr. Pierson's address on ' The Evangelisation of the World in this Generation ' was splendid. Is it not a wonderful thought that that is possible? We admired very much the way in which those young men conducted the whole thing, so earnestly and admirably, yet most modestly. The leaders all expect to be in the Foreign Field in a year. I am sure they will make splendid missionaries. A wonderful collection of £1,600, when £900 was asked for, was an object lesson for all the representatives of Missionary Societies of how the money can come in answer to prayer and proper teaching on the subject.''

During a visit to her old Belfast home, in the summer of 1896, Mary enjoyed the society of two of the most eminent women of our time, Mrs. Lewis and Mrs. Gibson of Cambridge. They were a very fascinating type for her, scholar-saints of her own sex. Regarding her intercourse with them she wrote a too brief note to Hélène. " We have with us two very learned ladies, who have come to take part in a Con- ference arranged by our Church. They have spoken in one of the largest Churches in Belfast, Fisherwick. They are twin-sisters, and they have made several journeys to the East in search of rare and ancient MSS. Four years ago they discovered at Sinai what is believed to be one of the oldest manuscripts of the Gospels, dating, it is thought, from the fourth century. They are very amiable and charming ladies, who not only answer all one's questions regarding their own studies, but at the same time interest themselves in all manner of things."*

A note written in the end of the same year shows how Mary was honoured among those who might almost be called her own people. " Two weeks ago I took the Y.W.C.A. meeting in Dungannon. I expected only girls and perhaps some of our friends, but found a great many others there. I cannot judge how the meeting went, but know that I waited on God for the subject and strength, so the result is certainly in His hands, not mine. Such a thing takes all the spare time of three or four days before. I should not like to have it often to do. It is good, though, to know a message so distinctly given. It makes one feel God so near and open to our cry and true to His promises." . . . And then the letter concludes very humanly. " Norah, David, some cousins, and I have been skating yesterday and to-day. The ice was lovely."

Whatever might be the character of the audience she expected, she always showed the respect due to it by coming with a definite and carefully thought out message. As a speaker on Foreign Missions, however, she became so full to overflowing with her theme that in the end she found it a positive benefit both to herself and her hearers if she left a good deal to the inspiration of the moment. This applied to the greatest audience of all, at the Annual Conference.

* Since these pages were written Mrs. Margaret Dunlop Gibson, D.D., LL.D., Litt. D., has ended her brilliant career as a Christian scholar.

"I was greatly pleased with the Zenana Day," she wrote after the General Assembly of 1905, "such a crowd seeming so anxious to get in. I was thankful I got on so well. I was not very nervous beforehand; purposely I did not prepare anything until the night before, for fear I should be turning it over and over in my mind and getting disgusted with it." Clearly in such a case it was good to remember the old precept, "Be not anxious how or what ye shall speak; for it shall be given you in that hour what ye shall speak."

Another letter shows her among her "ain folk" of the quiet countryside, ever welcome in kitchen or parlour. "I try," she writes to her Paris friend, "to visit all the girls of my Class in their homes. This takes time; I do one, or perhaps two visits in a day. They all live far out in the country—a walk of an hour and a half from here if one goes on foot. One day I dined at 12.30, and at 1.30 set out on my bicycle, to get back before five, when the day is almost done. Another day I started cycling at four, left the 'bike' in the post-office at Castlecaulfield, and went the rest of the way on foot. I asked for my tea in one of the farms at seven, and returned to Castlecaulfield, where there was a prayer meeting. I was convoyed (*accompagnée*) back by one of my old pupils, now married, with her husband carrying the baby. I assured them that I didn't fear to return quite alone, but the husband insisted. 'We'll take you past the old Castle; this woman (his wife) wouldn't like to go by it *her lone* at night.' Probably they did not believe my assurances that I was not afraid of the ghosts.''

The most striking feature of Mary's home life was its refined simplicity. She did not need the Apostle's dissuasion from the '' outward adorning of golden jewels and costly apparel,'' because she instinctively obeyed his great exhortation to seek '' the immortal beauty of a gentle and modest spirit.''* She never wore feathers or furs, hating the cruelty inseparable from both. The thought of millions of the loveliest birds being killed at the nesting time, and millions of furry creatures lying for days in steel traps with broken limbs, all to glorify a London or Paris season, haunted her like a Moloch sacrifice or the cruelties of vivisection. She had, it appears, some beautiful brooches, the gifts of friends, to which her husband added a diamond one as a wedding present. Unfortunately, some of the former got lost, and she expressed a fear that the latter also might go, so he at length gratified her by selling it that she might have the money to give away. To do this afforded her far more pleasure than the diamonds, and she bought herself a very inexpensive substitute. For the fugitive fashions of this world she could scarcely be said to care at all. Her '' simple life '' was no affectation. Call it the artlessness of an artist, or the instinct for '' the better part,'' at any rate it was a phase of her personal freedom, and her most discerning friends all loved her for being true to herself.

'' Some may think,'' writes her sister-in-law, Mrs.

* I Peter iii. 3. Dr. Moffatt's translation.

David Brown, "that it was easy for Mary Crawford to lead the life she did. She never knew the carking care that lack of means brings in its train; she lived among congenial friends; her lot was cast 'in a good land.' That is all true, and it only makes the simple austerity of her life and character the more striking. 'Mother is funny,' one of her little girls used to remark, ' she would rather walk than drive in the motor!' Simplicity ruled her mode of life—simplicity in dress, in food, in habits, in the equipment of her house. She indulged in scarcely any pleasures, except perhaps those of foreign travel, which do not lie within the reach of all. The beauties of sea and sky and countryside, the peace of home, the uplifting influence of music and literature, the activities of a life devoted to unselfish service, the companionship of children and kindred-spirited friends—these were the things which brought her happiness. But we felt in talking with her that there was always a detachment of spirit from worldly interests, an affection set on things which must have their counterpart in heaven."

When she was the mother of three children, Mary began a kind of Journal or *Manuscript,* as she called it, in which she continued to make entries from time to time for about fifteen years. The book extends in all to 150 pages, and records in a singularly lucid manner every trait of character she observed in her children from their infancy upward, every striking saying, every hopeful sign of progress, along with suggestions of her own for the correction of faults

WITH LAURENCE AND OLIVER

and the formation of good habits. It would not be fair to the young people to reveal the secrets of this family journal, but one early entry may be given as a specimen. " Each of the three children had, in infancy, a special preference—Laurence for Trees, Oliver for the Heavens, Alice for Music. When outside, Laurence was a little fretful; if you carried him under the trees he gazed up into the branches with pleasure. As he grew older, he was interested in the names of different trees, and soon learned to know several even in winter. When three or four years old, he was intensely interested, one Spring, in the opening of the buds. He asked me, ' But *how* do the leaves come out of those little buds? Is there a little door that opens to let them out?' Uncle David was going away to Palestine in February or early March, and Laurence said to him, ' When you come back the trees will all have leaves on them.' This he said as if announcing a wonderful, new event.

" As soon as Oliver could speak he made remarks about the heavenly bodies. One day when about three he said, ' The moon is far smaller than the stars, but it looks far bigger because it is nearer.' He said that Papa had told him this. He often remarked on the stars being very far away. One evening when out with me he said, ' I don't like the stars, they are too dark.' He soon learned to recognise the Plough. One day, when out driving, we had got to the top of a hill and saw a lovely sunset all over the sky. Oliver was *greatly* impressed, far more than Laurence. He was just gasping with admiration. A week or two later we called his attention to a sunrise to be seen from the window. He admired silently for a while, and then said to me, ' But, Mama, where is the other sky? ' He meant the whole sky-covering we had seen the other time.

" When Alice was only a month or two old, if I began to play the piano, she became quite still and listened. As soon as I stopped she was again full of life and activity, to stop still again when she heard the piano. I often laid her on the hearthrug and she would be quite happy while I played three or four pieces. Favourites were Mendelssohn's *Spring Song* and Heller's *Tarantelle*. At eight months, one day I was singing, and I heard her imitate three or four of the high notes. At a year and three or four months she could sing a tune quite correctly. Now, at two years and a month, she is not singing quite so much. She objects very much to sing when asked to, and this has been so all along. She knows two verses of *Qui dit au soleil,* and in several other French hymns gets hold of a word or two here and there."

All this is interesting not only for its insight into child minds—surprising little mirrors flashing unexpected lights for those who have eyes to see—but also as an index to the writer's own thoughts. It was just because trees, stars and music never ceased to thrill herself that she loved to observe their power over those who were fresh from the hand of God. She retained through life the child mind that sees miracles everywhere. " Tyrone among the bushes " is an admirable local phrase, and whether the bushes were clothed with emerald or dyed in russet and crimson, she had no difficulty in believing with Linnæus and Mrs. Browning that we may see "every common bush afire with God." "She revelled," says one of her missionary guests from the Far East, "in scenery, autumn colours, flowers, scents. That was why, if time permitted, she preferred walking—she got time to drink it all in. A garden was a delight to her, a place of rest and quiet, where God walked with her and renewed her."

It goes without saying that her classical music continued to give delight wherever she went. When her two eldest children were small boys she took them for a change to Rosapenna in Donegal. The hotel where they stayed was full of Ulster and Scotch folk, among the latter being an eminent Moderator of the National Church. An evening or two after her arrival Mary was asked by a friend to play to the two or three people who were in the drawing-room. As soon as she had begun, other guests came in, and yet others, until the room was filled. Every evening after that they all came with one desire, and she held them in rapt silence while she played to them the grandest music in the world, all from memory. Some of the listeners who recall those evenings after twenty years, speak of them as among the most charming in their lives.

Her spiritual growth was meanwhile all the steadier and surer because she was not over-anxious about it. The following words reveal a spirit as far removed from any morbid fears of backsliding as from foolish fancies of perfectionism. "I never heard of anyone reaching the zenith and then declining, and I don't believe in such a thing either. I believe we shall go on learning always to love God more to the end of our days. If it were not to be so, it would indeed be a sad case. At the rate of progress we make it would, I think, take a great many years to reach anything like the right thing. I have sometimes been troubled to think how little I grow in grace, but I don't mean to worry about that either. I think that is one of the things that belong more to the Lord than to me. ' No man by taking thought can add a cubit to his stature.' I think that belongs as much to the soul as to the body. I think my business is just to try and be faithful in all the little things about me. Dear me, that is hard, and I am constantly failing! But I believe it is my business never to give up—to be always ' forgetting the things which are behind and pressing on.' "

Equally wise and true is the following : " It often helps me wonderfully to think of God as the Creator. Not only has He made all I see, but He made me, He made you, He made our faculties and tendencies. He meant them all to tend to good, to Himself, but He knew the possibilities of evil arising from the very nobility of our nature, our free will. He prepared all the helps we need to lead and persuade us to give our wills up to Him. He gave Himself entirely for us, to provide a new heart, a new nature for us. All that is needed is just for us to be willing to accept it all."

CHAPTER VI

THE SOCIETY OF ENCOURAGERS

ONE of our Lord's favourite words, "Be of good cheer" (θαρσεῖτε), appears in the French New Testament as *Prenez courage*. Wherever it occurs it might be rendered by our single English word "Courage!" Christ was the Founder of the great Society of Encouragers, of which He is the ever-living President. Everyone who learns His secret becomes a Greatheart, who lives to make the weak strong and very courageous. One who knew Mary Crawford well in her youth says that her power consisted just "in what she believed her friend into doing or being. She had that knack to a wonderful degree. She never seemed to dream that others could not do what she did —almost as a matter of course. She could so lead one on, step by step, that one found oneself doing the impossible." Not long ago, when the newly-founded Irish Girls' Auxiliary to Foreign Missions needed a motto, and asked her to suggest a suitable text, she hesitated, knowing there were so many helpful ones, and then she said that one verse which had come to mean a great deal to her was, " I can do all things through Christ who strengtheneth me." The interpretation of these words seemed to her clear. " Surely they mean that with the call comes the enabling, even in the matter of a seeming impossibility." The heartening motto was unanimously adopted. In many minds it will always be associated with her who proposed it.

The Girls' Auxiliary, which now holds a secure place in the affections of the Church, had at first some difficulty in establishing its right to exist. People are slow to learn that no great cause can ever stir the enthusiasm of the young unless it offers them a partnership. "When the G.A. was younger," writes one who had been its Secretary, " and not very steady on its feet, it was being criticised as new societies sometimes are, and Mrs. Brown took up the cudgel on its behalf, metaphorically speaking. She explained that the G.A. merely meant that the girls were trying to do their bit after their own fashion; that girls liked to do things themselves, and were much happier and more natural if allowed to put their ideas into running a little branch, perhaps informally, instead of being asked to sit shyly, and probably silently, among older and more experienced folk. Coming at the beginning of the work, this will show what a deep, understanding sympathy Mrs. Brown had with young people, and how much she thought of the Girls' Auxiliary."

The same trait is described by Mary's cousin, Mrs.

Hamilton Martin, in a very engaging manner. " She was always, I think, fond of encouraging people to try to do what they imagined they could not do. My earliest remembrance of her is at Maine Mount, while I was there with Nellie and some of the others. Annie Crawford* and I were the wee ones. We were all jumping from a height on to some hay below. We two little ones were afraid to venture. Mary took hands and jumped with us to give us confidence, and then in a little we were able to do it ourselves. . . . It was the same when my husband, the boys, and I stayed at Agharainy in 1915 —Mary was there encouraging the children, never too busy to leave what she was at and attend to a child, finding something to occupy and interest each one.

" It was a great privilege to live at Mount Randal as I did when a girl. Mary took so much trouble to help me, and to her I owe more than I can tell. She had a very strong sense of duty, and many a time talked to me about it. She used to say that when we ought to do a thing God gave the power to do it. She taught me music, and gave me piano lessons as if that were her work. I remember her encouraging me, in trying to play something for people, by telling me that she used sometimes to feel when she sat down to play that she could not do it, and then she would recall the words, ' I can do all things through Christ.' "

Through her sons Mary came into touch with many other Irish lads at the most plastic time of their

* After serving as a Medical Missionary, she married the Rev. J. F. Steele, D.D., of Broach, India, whose recent death is mourned by the whole Church.

life. The average schoolboy has little taste for the dry dogmas of religion, but he quickly realises the power of a living faith, while he thrills to the magnetic influence of a Christian friendship. When Laurence and Oliver were senior boys at Dungannon Royal School, their mother took a warm personal interest in their comrades, whom she often invited to Agharainy. One of them, who has just completed his studies in Derry*, gives us an idea of the result. " It was to me," he says, " a great source of delight to go out to Mrs. Brown's house. Frequently I went as Oliver's special friend, but we used as well to go out in quite large numbers, and we invariably spent a very happy time. In a thousand and one ways she interested and fascinated us. We could not help being impressed by what we saw, and often we confessed this to each other. Above all things, boys don't like to be preached at. As a rule the schoolboy is extremely hard to get to talk about religious subjects. He has a horror of the ' goody-goody,' and while he has his own feelings and inward experiences he cannot bring himself to speak about them. Mrs. Brown understood boys. She never talked in a personal way, yet in her presence we instinctively felt that religion was a true and real thing, and that the Christian life was a life worth living. I think it was through her that I first really learned the meaning of the words ' beauty of holiness.' I remember a conversation that took place in the dormitory one night before ' Lights Out.' Our topic was

* W. Graham Mulligan, whose father was a missionary to the Indian Jungle Tribes, has volunteered for mission work in the land of his birth.

sincerity in religion. We had just been to Mrs. Brown's, and when we were closing the subject one boy said, ' If ever there was a real Christian, Mrs. Brown is one.' That just summed up what we thought of her.''

If she could thus make the higher life real and attractive to schoolboys, her gift for influencing and encouraging girls was naturally still more remarkable. In some of them she might see greater possibilities than others, but she endeavoured to draw out the best that was in every one she came in contact with. Often she discerned their real capacity when they had little idea of it themselves, and not a few who are to-day serving Christ at home or abroad think with gratitude of a sacred friendship which enabled them to realise the joy of whole-hearted devotion to His cause and Kingdom. The words of one of them will help to express the thoughts of many.

'' I remember,'' says the wife of a young Gujarat missionary, '' it was a cold bleak evening the first time I came to stay at Agharainy. Mrs. Brown had written that she would like me to come for a few days, that we might talk over Girls' Auxiliary plans. I had seen her twice before, but had never spoken to her. She was on the platform of the station to meet me. I was shy, and her words of welcome and her manner were very quiet. The youngest children and their Swiss governess were waiting in the porch to greet us. Everything looked cosy and inviting in the warm firelight and lamplight. The feeling of shyness, of being a stranger, was still

K

with me, and I just sat and listened to the free and merry talk. When all the children had gone to bed, she made me draw in my chair close to the fire, and *then* I felt I got near her; shyness fled, and soon I found myself telling her all about what we girls had been trying to do. I was to go the next day to speak for the first time at a meeting about the movement among the girls of our Church, and I was feeling so nervous and afraid. I told her what I meant to say; she listened, and suggested improvements and gave valuable hints. Then quietly she said, ' Let us pray about it '; so we knelt down, and I know those few, slowly-spoken sentences brought help and assurance to me. It was such a definite prayer, spoken just as if she were speaking to some one near, and I went upstairs feeling that I had got strength to go on with next day's ordeal. She came with me to the station in the morning, and as we walked up and down the quiet platform waiting for the train, she talked so cheerily and helpfully about doing God's work and how out of weakness we were made strong. When I got back the next day she was so kind and sympathetic and anxious to hear about everything. ' I was praying for you and remembering you often through the day,' she said, and I knew I had been held up by those praying thoughts of hers.

" She delighted in young people and entered so heartily into their lives. She once said, ' I feel there is *such a power* among the girls of our Church, if they are praying and working; we look for great things from this movement.' And it was that expecta-

tion, with the desire to do all she could to encourage
and develop the work, that made her have different
girls whom she knew to be interested at her house.
During those days with her, many felt not only that
they had got help and inspiration to go back and do
all they could for the Master's work, but that they
themselves had seen a fresh vision of Jesus Christ,
and that the example of her radiant companionship
with Him would have a lasting influence on their
lives.

"There were things that perplexed us, questions
that we couldn't have courage to ask others, but somehow we found ourselves asking her, and she would say,
'I'm glad you told me; I would like to help,' and
then the answers and the help would come. She was
then so intimate and unreserved; she would tell what
she herself had felt when she was a girl, and how
she got help. It was that delicate, beautiful under-
standingness which made it easy to tell her things.

"To one who had told her about a difficult problem
that had to be faced, she said, 'I was awake before
the dawn thinking about you, dear, and the decision
you must make.' She would not counsel the easiest
way, the path of least resistance. She believed that
the increasing years brought a corresponding increase
in responsibility. 'When I see a beautiful bud in the
garden' (we were passing a rosebush as she spoke)
'I rejoice over its loveliness, but if, when I come again
after a time, I found it still a bud, I should be disappointed. It ought to blossom and give out all its
sweetness round. To remain a bud would be to fail

in its life.' She would not counsel a definite course of action—she would not decide for one—but she gave the fruit of her experience, and directed one to something in God's Word that would be specially helpful, and left one to judge for oneself.

"Looking back now, it seems to me that she did not *talk* a great deal, but all she said was marvellously effective. One felt that her words were God-prompted. She did not always reply to a question at once, but the next day, or some time later, she would refer to it and give her opinion. In between, one knew that she had been praying it over and getting the help she sought. I am certain the secret of her power in her letters and conversation was her constant life in Christ. Once she said her life was so happy, so full of content in the companionship of Jesus, that she felt she had ' joy unspeakable '—those words alone expressed what she felt."

Last and perhaps best of all, Mary was the helper and encourager of little children. Her work among them was unwearied and lifelong. To begin with a matter which is more important than it may seem, she believed in developing the dramatic instinct which is in every child, and in her letters one lights upon several passages like the following : " Alice and Honor have been very busy over a play got up by Jessie Dickson of Dungannon,—Thackeray's *Rose and the Ring*. It came off last week, and was very good indeed. There were about thirty-five in the play—a great labour for Jessie. Alice was one of the principal characters, a little maid in a palace who turns out at the end to be a princess. She is quite unselfconscious, and throws herself into it all most thoroughly. Honor was an elf, and quite entered into that character.

> I am a little elf so brown,
> Sportive as the thistledown.

She danced about most sportively. It was all very pretty. I think it is good for the children to appear in public and so learn not to be shy. I do think shyness causes a terrible amount of suffering. Naturalness is so very desirable, and a capacity for doing something to entertain others."

One of the secrets of Mary's own magnetic power over children lay in her gift for making work appear to be play, a gift which is nearly allied to the faculty for changing law into gospel and prose into poetry. No one could ever doubt her faith in the virtue of real work. " I believe," she writes, " there is safety in work; it is one of our blessings and mighty helps. I think mind as well as body needs to be busy. I encourage this in my children all I can, to be busy, busy all the time, and to try to do something for others." But she wished to redeem all the work of little minds and hands from drudgery, in the spirit of God's Master Workman who is described as " rejoicing (the word means *playing* or *sporting*) always before Him."*

Knowing by instinct most of the ideas now commonly associated with the name of Madame Montessori, acting always on the advice which she loved to give to

* Proverbs viii, 30-31, R.V. Margin.

others, "Don't tell a child what not to do, tell it what to do," making education the skilful "drawing out" of what is in the learner's own mind, the artistic encouragement of his natural growth, and never forgetting the "highest reverence" which is due to the personality of every boy and girl, she could so enchain the interest and direct the teeming fancy of little folk as to make work seem to them the most delightful thing in the world.

All education seemed to her pitifully meagre which did not recognise the spiritual, Godward instinct as the crowning glory of every child's mind. She looked on faith, hope and love as flowers which cannot unfold too soon in the garden of the soul. Her minister at Castlecaulfield once said something to her about the early age at which divine things may become real to a child, when she quickly responded, "Oh, I am a great believer in that. One day, for instance, I was sitting in the garden when my little daughter came to me and said, 'Mother, what are you doing?' I replied that I was meditating. 'What is meditating?' she asked, and I told her it was thinking of God and of how good He is to us all. 'Well,' said she, 'I'll go and meditate too.' And, as she sat some distance from me, I could not but think God was just as much pleased with her meditation as with mine."

It was as the friend and encourager of little children that Mary came to feel, after long experience, that she had a kind of mission to improve and even to reform the Sunday School. She was a reader of the American *Sunday School Times,* and the stimulating ideas of that paper in regard to the grading of scholars and training of teachers chimed in with all that she had learned in the course of more than twenty years. After the opening of a new hall, with numerous classrooms, at Castlecaulfield, she introduced the new methods, and was delighted with the results. On Christmas Day, 1911, we find her writing : " At Sunday School I now have the Infant Class meeting in a nice big classroom and sitting in little arm-chairs. We had Mr. Jenkins, the Sunday School expert here, and he helped us to organise this, also to grade the whole school. These are things I had desired for a long time. I wanted an infant class where the poor little things would not have to sit and say catechism all the time. We have marching and action songs, and do all sorts of things. The children just love it. It is perfectly sweet to have their eyes fixed on one while one tells the story, and to get such ready response. They have not yet reached the stage where the height of good manners is to show no feeling whatsoever. Two or three senior scholars are assistants, and they often tell the story or take some other part in the proceedings."

On Sunday morning Mary always preferred to walk the two miles to Church, though others might drive. She went by a short way through the fields, carrying a little bag on her arm with all she needed for her lesson to the children. " It was a treat," says Mrs. Boyd, who accompanied her one morning, " to see her with the little ones; her love for them shone in her eyes, and her power of interesting them made the lesson full of charm and delight. That morning it was on part of Psalm i. She had drawn a large tree with spreading branches, growing beside a river. Her own children had got ready nine round apples cut out in paper, each one representing a fruit of the Spirit— Love, Joy, Peace, etc. The class learned the words :

> ' He shall be like a tree that hath
> Been planted by a river.'

' What kind of a tree,' she asked, ' is one that grows by a river?' The beauty, the freshness, and the shade were all described by the children, and the source of its strength. Then she asked what fruits God loves to see in us. The verse in Galatians was turned up and read aloud. Each child in turn came out and pinned on a fruit to the tree. One felt those children would *never* forget the spiritual fruits that the Christian must show in his life."

An eminent teacher of teachers, the late Dr. Maurice Paterson, of Moray House, Edinburgh—two of whose daughters have married Mary's brothers, James and William—summed up his impressions of her by saying, " She is a born educationist." This was so apparent to all who knew her that children of a larger growth were always glad to receive instruction and guidance from her. " Teaching," says Mrs. Boyd, " seemed just part of her. She delighted to help others to become proficient, and she had the rare power of making one enthusiastic. She would, for instance, explain fully the system on which she was taught the piano, entering into every detail and showing how the plan could be carried out. She sketched and painted

beautifully, and when we were out picnicking in the
April sunshine on the banks of a lake, she provided
pencil and paper and showed how to set about sketching from nature. It was an education to be with her;
yet it wasn't that she set out to teach—it was just as if
she guided one—it was the natural outcome of her own
clear beautiful way of understanding things, and
mastering them, and wanting to make others share in
her riches."

Mary's own sources of inspiration and encouragement did not change. In addition to her faith they were
chiefly three—Nature, friends old and new, and good
news from India and China. Natural scenery appealed
not only to her five senses, but to that sixth sense
which is the gift of the artist and the mystic. Once,
when she and her brother Willy were climbing and
sketching together among the mountains of North
Wales, they went into a cottage and had lunch. " The
man of the house," she relates, " was good company.
He could not make out why people come there in such
large numbers from all parts. ' What is there to
see? ' he asked. I laughed and could not well explain
it to him." She did not tell him that we go through the
world seeing what we have the gift of seeing, or that
the voices of Nature awaken echoes of something
greater in our own souls; but her picturesque narrative
indicates that she and her brother enjoyed to the full
" the swift torrents, the ferns and heather, the rocks
and oaks and firs " of the Carnarvon mountains.

Many more of her letters contain travel pictures.

Now we find her " sitting among the heather and brackens of the Trossachs, reading aloud *The Lady of the Lake*"; now at Bundoran, " in front of a charming view of sea and rock and mountain, making the quest of health just now my main occupation "; now at Innsbruck, in Tyrol, where " it is wonderful to walk down a handsome street and see a great mountain towering at the end of it, walk down another and see another mountain at the end of it "; now at Ste. Croix, above the Lake of Neuchâtel, looking across a sea of cloud to the glistening Alps beyond, and watching the exquisite sunset; now approaching Davos, where " the way up is most lovely—the train climbs, climbs, climbs along the side of the mountains, while chalets, green pastures, and rushing torrents are seen far below."

But Nature spoke nowhere more intimately—more " to her heart," as a Hebrew poet would have said— than among the fields and woods beside her own Irish home. There are many references in her letters to solitary walks to and from Dungannon, not by the broad highway but along the narrow winding lanes, and perhaps it is these walks, more than anything else, that seal her as a mystic. She felt what thinkers reason about—the spiritual principle in Nature. The outer world, with all its glorious forms and colours, stood in some deep and vital relation to her own soul. " An out-of-doors prayer," she writes, " is *so* helpful to me. The beauties of Nature around help me so, speak to me of the beauty of holiness, the glory, purity, and goodness of God." " She told me," says one of her missionary friends*, " that when she went out walking, as she loved to do, she just talked with God as if He were walking by her side as her companion. This natural uplook of her spirit to God was, it seems to me, that which gave such charm and power to her life."

There is no evidence, however, that Mary ever felt the seduction of a purely contemplative life, or let herself be absorbed in her own spiritual emotions. When she " went away by herself alone "—the words recall the highest Example—it was always that she might restore her soul for the life of action. She thus represented that finest of all Christian types, the practical mystic— Mary and Martha in one—whose life is summed up in two things, a great love and much serving. To a dear friend whom she knew to be fighting a brave battle with temptation we find her writing : " Yesterday I walked in to and out from Dungannon—my main errand was to pray for you."

How practical her sympathy always was might be indicated in many ways. Her public spirit was ever adding to the circle of her fellow-workers and friends. Along with her husband she took a very deep interest in all questions of hygiene, especially in the latest ideas as to the treatment of tuberculosis. Some of her letters deal almost entirely with health lectures, health exhibition, health visitors, and the like. She could never forget what she owed to one of the great doctors of Paris, and she longed to see the poorest in Ireland enjoying all the benefits that science can confer on the

* Rev. James M'Cammon, Manchuria.

sick and suffering. This brought her into touch with the Countess (now the Marchioness) of Aberdeen, who, with the Lord Lieutenant, did a great work for the improvement of the health of Ireland. A Women's National Health Association was founded, the objects of which were—" to arouse public opinion, and especially that of the women of Ireland, to a sense of responsibility regarding the public health; to spread the knowledge of what may be done to guard against disease, and to eradicate it when it appears; and to promote the upbringing of a healthy and vigorous race." The Association, as its latest report shows, still continues its beneficent labours in all the four provinces of Ireland, and a Dublin minister* says truly of its foundress : " *Inter alia,* she has been the preserver from early death of thousands of my countrymen and women by her campaign against tuberculosis."

Lady Aberdeen visited Belfast at the beginning of her ten years' work in Ireland (1905-15), and was for some days the guest of Sir William and Lady Crawford. Mary was in her old home to meet her, and common sympathies and aims drew them together. Into the subsequent health campaign Mary threw herself with all her heart and soul. Lady Aberdeen writes in warm terms of the deep interest which Mr. and Mrs. Brown took in the work of the Association, both in their own district and in connection with an Irish Village which was organised at one of the great Exhibitions in London. " In this way," she adds, " I continued

* Rev. J. D. Osborne, D.D., Rutland Square.

to hear from them from time to time, and all my impressions of Mrs. Brown, formed on the occasion of my first meeting her at her father's house, were always strengthened in admiration of the high ideals which she and her husband pursued in all they undertook."

Mary had yet another source of encouragement, for " as cool water to a thirsty soul, so is good news from a far country." The lands of which she loved best to hear were India and China. In the autumn of 1906 she tells Hélène of a great inspiration which she received during a visit to Mount Randal. " Sir Andrew Fraser, with his wife and two boys, were there. He is Lieutenant-Governor of Bengal, Willy's chief. On Sunday he gave addresses on Indian Missions in two of the principal Churches—Rosemary Street and Fisherwick. He speaks admirably. It is good to hear a man who governs fifty millions speak so religiously and so heartily about Missions." One can imagine how deeply she was moved when she heard him choose as his text in the former church, " Who is willing to consecrate his service this day unto the Lord? " and give this testimony : " I am not a missionary, nor have I any secular connection with missions. I am a Government official. I have lived thirty-five years in India, and in the discharge of my duties have travelled throughout the whole of that great country, and have had exceptional opportunities of knowing it and its people very intimately. Whenever I came across Christian mission work I looked into it; I visited mission schools, mission hospitals, mission churches, and everywhere I saw splendid work going on. I came to see that the same Holy Spirit who guided Paul in the methods he should use in his mission work is still guiding the missionaries into wise and far-reaching plans." Then he gave "examples out of hundreds," all showing "that missions in India are a great success, that God is gathering out for Himself a great people there, and that one day that country will be won for Him."

China was now peculiarly dear to Mary, as the land of modern martyrs, where her brother Alek and his brave wife were labouring amid many dangers. In the Spring of 1908 she was thrilled by the best news an editor ever received from the Far East—the report of a modern Pentecost. "The dawn," she told her readers, "is brightening in China. The native Christians are receiving such an outpouring of the Holy Spirit, they have been cleansed and strengthened and fitted for bringing others into the Kingdom."

Number after number of *Woman's Work* contained tidings akin to the following, which were received from Mrs. Hunter of Kwangning : "A spirit of prayer was poured out, and then it just seemed that men and women could no longer hold themselves back from the Lord, as if they were constrained to empty themselves of all sin and receive the Holy Spirit. There was something almost awesome about it all—to see great, strong, hard-looking men quivering, and in voices full of deepest agony confess their sins, and supplicate for mercy and pardon—not one, nor two, nor three, but large numbers—kneeling, aye, grovelling on the ground, beating their breasts and saying just a few

significant words—' Lord have mercy,' ' Pity me, O
Lord.' It was the agony of travail, giving birth to a
new soul. . . . And everything seems changed
since we have received the Holy Spirit. Old things
are passed away. Everything seems renewed : new
life, new love, a new spirit of prayer—prayer for
others, prayer for those who do not yet know Christ."

In the following spring Mary listened to one of the
Manchurian missionaries, Mrs. Keers of Chinchow, telling the General Assembly the whole wonderful story
over again, and concluding with the words : " Those
soul-stirring scenes have been indelibly stamped upon
my memory. They were indeed days of the Holy Spirit's
power, and we realised, as never before, something of
the meaning of the second chapter of the Acts. I say in
all humility, and yet it is true—that they have added a
richness and a fulness to my own spiritual life for
which I am deeply grateful to Almighty God." And
as Mary listened, she prayed for her own country.
When the petition " God save Ireland " shall at last
be answered, it will be in just such a way as that.
There can be no other.

Mary had partly shared the fear that China might
become, as she said, " a modernised heathen strong
nation." In that case, " what a terror to the world it
may be ! " But she became convinced that the martyr
spirit will be victorious there as everywhere, and that
China will yet take its place among the greatest
Christian nations. When she was a delegate to the
Edinburgh Missionary Conference of 1910 she was
thrilled by an address delivered by Dr. Arthur Smith,

of Pekin.   " He speaks," she wrote, " with enthusiasm of his beloved China, the triumphs of Christ there, and the possibilities of the future. Earnestness and humour kept the hearers spellbound. After the service a lady, speaking to him in the vestry, said she was sorry to read in the papers of more riots in China.   ' Riots ! ' he said, ' oh, we have crops of them in China, like turnips.   We don't mind them ; we are used to that sort of thing.   We were all killed in 1900.' "   Mary adds : " It reminds one of ' We are killed all the day long' ; 'as dying, and behold we live.' Missionary life in the present day in many ways reminds one of Paul's."   At last it is the all-daring, open-eyed missionary, not the arm-chair critic, who illuminates the Apostle's triumphant words, " We glory in tribulation also, knowing that tribulation worketh patience, and patience experience, and experience hope."

CHAPTER VII

THE FELLOWSHIP OF SUFFERING

" To make up the harmony of the world, the youthful death of the very bright and the very brave is not only necessary but a precious element. Glorious sorrow is as necessary, is as priceless as the nightingale or the evening star." *

" While psalmist, poet, and prophet in the Old Testament are continually troubled by the problem of suffering, ever returning to it, and never completely satisfied, the New Testament shows, for the most part, a complete unconsciousness that such a problem exists. In the New Testament, suffering is no longer a problem but a source of light, no longer a thing to be avoided, but a privilege to be claimed; and that because it is something shared by God Himself, and the means of His accomplishing the sublimest of all ends. God so delights in perfecting His creation, with all its beauty, by making it as complete morally as it aesthetically, that He thinks any sacrifice, no matter how tremendous, whether on His own part or on the part of His children, to be well worth while."†

* *The New Elizabethans,* p. 383.
† *God and the Struggle for Existence,* pp. 30, 33, 201.

Laurence Crawford Brown, the eldest of a family o
five, was born at Agharainy on October 5, 1894. Th
child " Lala," as his brother Oliver called him, i
remembered as a merry little fellow with a twinkle i
his eye and up to all kinds of pranks. His love of fu
showed itself very early. " When two years old," w
read in his mother's *Manuscript*, " he often asked to b
carried when out, complaining of being tired.
remember one day, when he was beseeching his fathe
to carry him, the latter said, ' You've not a bit of pit
for poor Papa.' This phrase amused Laurence, an
he repeated it several times and laughed. Another da
I saw him carrying a small doll on his shoulder an
saying, ' Not a bit of pity for poor Lala ! ' "

When he was six he got a little baby sister, an
after she had grown a bit, Mother said to him one day
" Go and bring baby to me, Laurence. Carry her ver
carefully." He ran away and came back with a kitte
in his arms, which he held out gravely to Mothe
" What nonsense," she sa'd, " I asked for baby.
" But you did not say which baby, Mother. How wa
I to know which one you wanted ? "

" From the first," says the MS., " Laurence ha
been lively, active, energetic. His fondness for Olive
did not prevent a great deal of teasing. Thoug
Oliver complained and sometimes cried, he preferre
Laurence's company. One day Laurence had bee
troublesome, and when he went out of the room I sai
to Oliver, ' Now we'll have peace, and he won't teas
us.' Oliver ran to the door and called, ' Come an
tease us ! ' "

Lala inherited all his mother's love of Nature. One morning in bed, after enquiring whether or not the window had been open all night, he said, " I like the breeze and the little birds singing." Words could not better express the spirit of Laurence's whole life.

He early showed a great fondness for martial hymns, his favourite when he was about six being " Hold the Fort." One day his mother explained two lines of a different kind of hymn—

> Frail children of dust
> And feeble as frail,

and the boys were interested in what she said of human frailty. Next day another military hymn was chosen, containing the swinging lines—

> Like a mighty army
> Moves the Church of God,

and Mother explained the Church as God's people. " Why mighty? " asked Laurence, in a tone of surprise. " Sure, you said people are feeble." A mighty army, and yet frail children of dust—can they be one and the same? Is it all prophetic?

Lala's love of animals also revealed itself very early. A lady who heard that *Black Beauty* was a favourite lent *Beautiful Joe*. The first part of this story is very sad, being about a poor little dog cruelly ill-used. Lala's father begins to read it one evening, but has to stop, Lala begging him not to go on. That night the child lies awake long, troubled by thoughts of poor

Joe. A cheerier story, a Bible one, is begun to him, and his spirit soon passes into the quiet land of oblivion.

Soon afterwards Lala delivered his maiden speech. The idea of it was suggested to him by a large card which his mother had got printed with the announcement of " A Lecture by Rev. A. R. Crawford," who had come home from China on his first furlough. This interested Laurence very much, and he was observed writing out a similar notice of " A Speech by Laurence Brown." Oliver whispered to his mother, " Laurence's speech will be on Kindness to Animals." Next morning Laurence remarked that he could not sleep for thinking of his speech. In the afternoon his audience, to the number of about twelve, assembled in the yard, and Laurence directed Frank, the stable boy, to bring Jenny, the donkey. Then he mounted a low wall and began in a steady voice : " You should always give horses and donkeys water to drink and hay in the rack, and you should always be kind to animals, and when they won't go on you should not beat them, but just say Clk ! Clk ! " Here there was a pause, during which Grannie started a clap. Then the speaker turned to the subject of rabbits, and briefly described their daily course of eating, playing and sleeping. Then with a sudden " That's all ! " he descended from the rostrum.

" For a good while," as we learn from the faithful MS., " Laurence objected to saying his prayers," but the writer adds : " Both boys are very impressible by religious teaching when taken at impressible moments." When Rev. xxi. was read to Laurence, and the Lamb's Book of Life explained, he added that night to his ordinary prayers, " Please write my name in Your Book." The chapter interested him greatly, the precious stones being very attractive to him. One day his mother took him to the Free Library in Belfast, and showed him a fine collection of precious stones. He looked at them with much delight, and that night wanted to have the chapter read over again to him.

" I am sometimes surprised," says the first and best teacher of the two lads, " to find how well they listen to Bible reading, but one thing I have noticed—it is of no use to read out of a shabby little Bible; they wriggle away and say, No, they don't want the Bible. Yesterday I took one of the nice large ones with good print which I got for a wedding present, and read John xxi., all but the last piece about Peter's death. They listened quite attentively, and Laurence answered questions about Peter's denial and the reason for the three times repeated question ' Lovest thou me? ' Then they asked for more." There was no lack of attractive Sunday books in their home, but when Laurence was seven and knew a good many of them, he remarked to his mother—" with much feeling," she notes—" The Bible is the nicest Sunday book." His favourite Old Testament stories at that time were about walls—the fall of the walls of Jericho, Nehemiah building the walls of Jerusalem, etc. His mother always found it better to read Bible tales in the language of Scripture than to make them simple in her own, for the boys were more interested. And she used to advise parents to read the stories to their little ones after they were tucked in bed and getting ready to sleep, in order that the great truths might form their last waking thoughts and have a good chance of mingling with their dreams.

When Laurence was eight his mother took him and Oliver to France for a couple of summer months. With their uncle Harry and Hélène Wehrlin, they stayed in a house at La Malmaison, about an hour's run from Paris by train. It was arranged that the boys should go to school with the children of the Protestant Pastor of the place, a boy and girl of about their own age. They had thus the chance of learning French in what their mother regarded as the only natural way of acquiring a knowledge of any foreign language, not grammar first, the writing of sentences second, and conversation last, but exactly the opposite order. The boys came home able to talk French fluently, and while they could not yet write it, that came with comparative ease later on. It was characteristic of their mother that she should wish the children of other parents to enjoy similar advantages, and this led her, years afterwards, as we shall see, to formulate and carry through an original and daring scheme to give the boys and girls of Dungannon Royal School all the benefits of foreign travel.

As Laurence grew up his mother and he were much together, and always agreeably occupied, whether at home or out of doors. He was in

his twelfth year when she wrote in her MS. :
"Laurence enjoyed very much taking bicycle rides
with me; we explored many roads before unknown
to him. We generally made a picnic. He would like
very much to go to Switzerland, and we keep that
before us as a treat to look forward to."

Again she writes : "From Christmas to Easter I read
Jules Verne's *L'Ile Mystérieuse* to Laurence. He
enjoyed it immensely. He often reads in French to me
while I sew."

He was educated first at Clanrye School, Belfast,
then at the Royal School, Dungannon, and the in-
fluences surrounding him in both were the best. He
worked diligently and did his teachers credit. He
loved Donaghmore and all its people, and looked
forward with happiness to his life-work there. The
centre of his thoughts was always his home and its
dear ones. His first question on returning after an
absence would be, "Mother, have you anything you
want done?" So the small repairs to bells, locks
and furniture were put off till he came home. He
was not quite so devoted to books as Oliver, who was
preparing for Cambridge when the war broke out,
but holiday seasons spent in France and Germany
gave them both an excellent knowledge of the
languages of these countries. One of these trips
abroad, in the summer of 1909, when the elder brother
was nearly fifteen, is referred to in their mother's MS.
"Laurence and Oliver came with me to London,
where they spent ten days before going to Germany.
They travelled alone from London to Dresden, where

they were met by Eve Bahmann, daughter of the Pastor of Skassa, who took them on to the Erzgebirge. Two weeks or so they spent there, and six weeks at Skassa. The boys enjoyed it all very much, and got on well with German, writing home frequent and interesting letters, often in German. Two or three days in London ended the holiday, and they came home looking well, both of them broader and stronger."

From Dungannon School Laurence went to the Technical College, Belfast, for a two-years course of engineering, and finally, when nineteen, he started for Chicago, where he was to be employed for other two years in the office of the Inland Steel Company. Of his departure for America and his life there his mother wrote : " We had lovely talks, and I felt no fear at seeing him go off. Friends asked, ' Are you not afraid of letting your son go to such a dreadful city as Chicago? ' I knew Laurence's feet were firm on the Rock, and I was not afraid. Living with Mr. W. Sloane, he attended Church and Bible Class and Y.M.C.A., so his spare time was well occupied. He enjoyed his experience, and got on well. His services were appreciated. He wrote lovely letters. He stayed one year, and would have remained a second, but when he heard Oliver had joined for the war, he said he did not wish the *little* brother to have *all* the spunk. So he came home."

Laurence saw his duty to Ireland and the Empire, and would not hold back, though war was utterly abhorrent to him. Eager for the right, and burning with patriotism, he also saw everything through eyes of faith. His first thoughts are expressed in a letter of Sunday, August 9, just after the declaration of war. " What will heathendom think when it sees the greater part of the professed followers of the Prince of Peace using every means in their power to destroy one another? But the Lord of Hosts reigns; He cannot err, and must have some wise purpose behind it all. We can only do our duty, and pray that in His mercy the days of affliction may be shortened."

Laurence was now nearly twenty. Between him and his mother there was perfect confidence and abounding sympathy. He had become, as she afterwards wrote, " the most loving and darling big son anyone could wish to have. And Robert was beginning to lean on him, young, strong, clever, intensely interested in all his schemes, ready with ideas of his own."

Motoring was Laurence's chief amusement, and he was a very skilful driver. " Soon after his return," the writer of the MS. continues, " he motored his father, Aunts Mary and Norah, and me on a lovely tour round Ireland. Kells, Howth, Newrathbridge, Enniscorthy, Lismore, Maryborough were the places where we stayed a night. In Lismore we spent a most lovely week-end. All the time the weather was perfect. The Rock of Cashel I shall never forget." Laurence was not much given to analysing his feelings, but in his own land and among his own people he clearly realised to the full the glory of living.

The war was a test of loyalty and a touchstone of character. There was, alas! ro conscription in Ireland, but none was needed in patriotic homes. While Laurence and Oliver quickly made their own decisions, they were helped by the knowledge that their action had their parents' warm approval—that, in Laurence Binyon's glorious words, " Love with the shining eyes the hard way chose." " I remember," writes Oliver, " the last evening before I went off to Omagh to enlist. Mother and I sat together; she read out of the Bible; what she read and what exactly she said I forget, but the atmosphere, and the spirit of her tender words of counsel and encouragement, are with me still. Some men whom I know, shrank from going home on leave, because of the inevitable parting again, but Laurence's and mine, though painful, were made very much lighter for us by the cheerful face both Mother and Father put on it."

Laurence had his training at Ballykinlar and Newry, Oliver at Aldershot and Eastbourne. In the spring of 1915 both were ready to go with the Ulster Division to France in the R.A.M.C. Just before they went they got six days' leave, and after the parting their mother wrote to her Norwegian friend Emma Thomas : "We grieved to see them go off to-day, and yet we are proud of them. We should be unhappy if they were not brave enough to offer. . . . Both belong to the Soldiers' Christian Association, and tell me about their meetings in camp. There are many faithful and good soldiers, though many are careless and godless. I often think this war is allowed to punish the people for selfishness and godlessness. But God has His great designs of mercy through it all."

2ND LIEUT. LAURENCE C. BROWN,
ROYAL INNISKILLING FUSILIERS,
FELL NEAR YPRES 16TH AUGUST, 1917, IN HIS 23RD YEAR.

Laurence served for a year and a half before he obtained a commission. Oliver never sought one, preferring the experiences of a private during all his five years in khaki. The work the two brothers were required to do in France must often have been very uncongenial, but neither of them ever said it was hard. Their command of French frequently enabled them to solve little difficulties that arose between their compatriots and the French peasants. Best of all, they never forgot in the army that they were soldiers of Christ. Captain Jaspar Robinson, a Wesleyan Chaplain, wrote to their father : " They always helped me in my work with the men, and their example was highly effective. I don't think I have met two brothers who stand out so prominently in my thoughts for all noble qualities."

On being recommended for a commission as an infantry officer, Laurence came home for training in the Cadet Camp, and returned to France in February, 1917. He was sent up to report for duty with the 8th Battalion of the Royal Inniskilling Fusiliers. On June 7 he took part in the battle of Messines, of which he wrote a graphic description. " It was the sight of a lifetime. From a spectacular point of view it was absolutely astounding. The night was mild and peaceful, everything apparently quite normal—an occasional shot, and a ' Verey ' light here and there. Then, without the slightest warning, at 3.10, four or five big mines on our front went up, throwing columns of earth, mingled with flame, hundreds of feet high. At the same time our artillery and machine-guns opened

with a deafening roar the most intense bombardment
that has ever been known, and our attacking waves
went forward. The Boche did not attempt to fight,
and I don't blame him. It's marvellous how anything
lived, yet a number of dugouts were found standing.
The whole earth was completely pulverised; not a
square yard was left that had not been shelled and
re-shelled. We saw lots of ' tanks ' go up, crawling
along like weird reptiles. It looked most amusing to
see the officer in charge walk out in front, reconnoitre a
few yards ahead, then beckon to the ' creature ' to
come on, which obeyed like a pet dog ! It seemed a
wonderful sensation to be able to walk about in ' No
Man's Land,' as if one were on the lawn at home,
when twelve hours previously it would have been sheer
suicide; and to stand on the parapet, where at one time
to show one's head over was asking to get a bullet
through it. As the day went on, streams of prisoners
were brought in. I didn't get much time to talk to
them. One chap I spoke to—he was helping to carry
down one of our wounded—told me he was an
' aspirant,' which corresponds to cadet, I think.
He was only eighteen, and had the Iron Cross, which
he had won on the Russian front. He wasn't sorry to
be done with the war, and he said he thought it was
' alles mit dem Vaterland kaput ' (all up with the
Fatherland)—that our attack was ' kolossal' ! Everyone agrees that we have a lot to be thankful for, when
one sees the strength of the positions captured, which
resisted all attacks for two-and-a-half years, and
realises that it might easily have been a repetition of

what the Ulster Division got last July. There is great
cause to praise God."

But in that middle year of the war the Allies had
many grave reverses and very heavy losses. Tragedy
was not softened by becoming universal, and many a
sympathetic nature seemed to feel the inrush of—

Desperate tides of the whole great world's anguish
Forced thro' the channels of a single heart.

To a friend Mary wrote a profoundly thoughtful letter.
"The newspapers in these times make sad reading.
It seems as if calamities were hanging over us. I read
The Revelation, and comfort myself with Jesus conquering and to conquer. The victory is His, but we
must pass through many tribulations." Then comes
a singularly poignant apocalyptic note. There is no
prayer for Divine intervention like a mother's heart-
cry, which is most irrepressible just when the present
spiritual union with Christ is most intimate. "Don't
you wish," asks this mother, "that Jesus would come
one of these days and put an end to so many horrors?
In the meantime it is grand and heart-satisfying to
have Him near, near, very near." To her and many
another mother, united in a great fellowship of suffering, Christian faith was returning in its original form,
which is not so much a passionate hope as a rapturous
assurance that the Kingdom of Christ, or rather
Christ in His Kingdom, will *somehow* break in upon
the present unbearable world-order and make all
things new.

Laurence's letters of that spring and summer give

vivid little pictures of an officer's daily life in the danger zone. A few extracts will suffice to show him as he always was—smiling, high-hearted, indomitable.

March 27 (to his mother) : "On Sunday evening I went with some others to a service conducted in a Y.M.C.A. hut by Major-General Simms and Dr. Park, whose address was very good. I spoke to Dr. Park after the service and he was very hearty. The place where it was held does not get many shells, though they had sent over a few a day or two before, one of which hit close to the Y.M., smashing a hut where we had been billeted the previous day."

April 9 : "We have an Intelligence Officer attached to us, an Oxford man and quite a scholar, who reads his Greek Testament regularly. I play him at chess pretty often. Thanks for the *Witness, Missionary Herald,* and *Tale of Two Cities.* The last I had read before, but I'll pass it on to someone else."

May 4 : "It is no hardship at all being in trenches in weather like this. In the mornings the birds, nightingales, larks, cuckoos, etc., give us a concert, aeroplanes also assisting. We don't have feet inspection now, as there is no danger of trench feet. It used to be rather funny going round, peeping into dugouts, which are very small in these parts, to see half a dozen pair of feet struggling towards the light. Ask one chap why he did not rub his with oil. 'Oh, they aren't mine, sir ! '"

May 15 : "The country is looking lovely, and nature seems trying to cover up the scars of war. ' No Man's Land ' is marked by a bright green patch, though on either side the ground is so much ploughed up by shells that nothing grows. It's funny to see sparrows building nests in trees on which there is hardly a branch."

May 20 : "There is no need to worry yourselves about me. All our affairs are in God's hands, and He has given us every reason to trust Him. Everyone here is very optimistic about the prospects this summer. *On les aura!* " (We'll have them!—words often on the lips of the Poilus.)

June 6 (to his father) : " I suppose you are at the Assembly this week. Please thank Uncle Alek for *Herald* and *Daybreak*. I was greatly interested in the report of the revival meetings in India."

June 16 : " We are having a fine rest in a lovely country place. It is a relief to get away from the continual pounding of the guns, and have nice green fields and hedges instead of dusty roads and the wilderness of torn-up earth."

June 23 (to Honor) : " The other night we had a gas alarm. Wakened up by gongs and church bells, we got our respirators on, but it turned out to be a false alarm. The inhabitants have all got masks (*gagoules*), and even the army horses. I don't know whether these have gas drill often! "

July 10 : " Many thanks for *Ballygullion* and *Silas Marner*. Please go steady, for I'm not half through *Adam Bede* yet."

July 20 : " I had an interview with an Intelligence Officer the other day. He conversed a bit in French and German, and got me to read some handwriting. He gave me to understand that I'd do."

Aug. 2 : " I hope you have not been too apprehensive lately on my behalf, because there was really no reason to be. You will have seen that there has been a successful advance. We have had a spell of awful weather the last couple of days, continuous rain turning everywhere into a quagmire. It must have been awfully trying for the poor troops up at the line. I'm extremely fortunate to be comfortably housed in a tent, though occasionally there is a small stream running through it."

July 31 was the beginning of the most cruel time for the 16th (Irish) Division. Laurence's Chaplain, Rev. Capt. W. T. M'Connell, of Markethill, speaks of it as " the slaughtering-time, which is covered by that name of awful import, Passchendaele." The weather broke on the very day of the advance to which Laurence refers above, and the words of the Canadian poet tell the rest : " It isn't the Huns and it isn't the guns, it's the mud, mud, mud." The tanks could not be moved forward, the aeroplanes had difficulty in getting up to reconnoitre, the " pill-boxes " could not be cleared out, and the gallant Irish were compelled to retire from the position which they had taken. Lt.-Col. Walkey, the commanding officer of Laurence's battalion, says : " In all my twenty-five months out there, those first eighteen days of August were far and away the most awful, for we accomplished but little and our battalion lost about 490 men and twenty officers. But all went through it cheerfully and courageously, like the fine fellows they were." According to Sir Philip Gibbs, " the losses in many of the battles amounted almost to annihilation to many battalions, and whole divisions lost as many as 50 per cent. of their strength after a few days in action."

Before Laurence's return to France his father had urged him to apply for Intelligence work, as capable men were badly wanted, and he had all the qualifications. But it was a safe job, and he would not ask for it. One day some of his brother officers were talking of him, and a senior man remarked, " If that boy had pushed himself forward as many do, he would have been far up in the Intelligence before now." In the end his abilities could no longer be overlooked. So valuable was the information he was able to gather by going in and out among the German prisoners of war, that the authorities decided to send him to the Intelligence Department.

But not yet. In a brief letter to his mother, written on the eve of another advance, Laurence says : " I am still with the battalion, and may be for some little time." For the past fortnight the battle-line had been under torrential rain. " Our men," writes Gibbs, the realist, " were never dry. They were wet in their trenches, and wet in their dug-outs. They slept in soaking clothes, with boots full of water, and they drank rain with their tea and ate mud with their bully." But that was at length passing, and with his never-failing optimism Laurence assures his mother that " it is now sunny and breezy, so that things are drying splendidly." For a moment his heart turns

M

away from grim scenes of war to the dear
commonplaces of home, where he is glad to have
learned that " the crops are looking well and the
fruit-picking progresses." Then with a " love to all,"
he lays down his pen. Among all the thousands of Irish
lads whose names are on the Roll of Honour, there
was no sweeter nature and no more gallant heart.

" On August 14," writes Capt. M'Connell,
" the 8th Inniskillings went once more into the front
line, preparatory for the attack. Laurence, who had
' stuck it ' splendidly all through, was now appointed
signalling officer. Lt.-Col. Walkey said of him,
' I knew he would do his work with all his heart. He
was a quiet boy, and never said much, but he was a
good officer, and he could keep his head.' At 4.45 on
August 16, the 16th Division went over the top,
making for an objective about two miles ahead. We
were supported by divisions on either flank, the Ulster
being on our left. Soon it became known that
we were held up at Borry Farm, which was only
about 200 or 300 yards in front of us. Before it could
be definitely said that there was a ' hold-up,' Laurence
was sent out with a few signallers to report on the
situation as far as he could learn what it was. Borry
Farm proved impregnable to infantry. The Bosches
sniped from it all day, concentrating especially on
officers, whom they could more easily detect by their
uniforms."

As Laurence led the signallers forward two
of them were killed. He was about fifty yards in

front of the others, when a sniper's bullet passed through his cheeks. He steadied himself, and raised his right hand to wave his men onward, when another bullet struck him in the body, and he fell. As soon as it was known that he was hit, his servant Hugh Finlay, a Newtownards man, with a bravery which won him the Military Medal, made his way through intense machine-gun fire to where Laurence lay, only to find that life had fled. Finlay afterwards said of his master, who had always treated him rather as a friend than a servant, " He was one of the coolest officers under shell-fire I ever knew. I think he had no fear." On a card in Laurence's Bible the words were found written in his own hand, " I sought the Lord and He heard me, and delivered me from all my fears."

All that was mortal of Laurence lies somewhere between Ypres and Passchendaele. Many a corner of those fields—to adapt the thought of Rupert Brooke's fine sonnet—is for ever Ireland. But in many cases there is no knowledge of the place where the sacred dust reposes. No cross was raised, no name inscribed. Had it been possible, Finlay would have faced the shell-fire a second time in order to bring his master's body into headquarters, but, to his great sorrow, he was compelled to retire with the battalion almost as soon as he got back to his dug-out. So Laurence had neither coffin nor shroud, neither burial service nor " Last Post." " The Graves Department," as his father writes, " told us that he was buried, but the spot was not located. " This did not," he pathetically adds,

" vex his mother—to her the earthly part was very little."

Her heart was with her treasure, elsewhere than in the shell-torn wilderness. Her faith finds expression in two letters, the first a very tender one to her own mother. " Of late years especially I always felt he was a bright angel, and he is certainly one now. Goodness filled his heart and shone out from him. He beheld as in a glass the glory of the Lord, and was changed into the same image. We give thanks for those nearly twenty-three years of love and beauty. I often read Luke i : ' Thou shalt have joy and gladness, and many shall rejoice at his birth. He shall drink no wine nor strong drink, and he shall be filled with the Holy Spirit even from his mother's womb.' He was the child of many prayers, yours and father's and others'. We asked for the Holy Spirit for him, and he turned to God as a flower to the sun."

To a dear friend she wrote : " Often when he sat beside me in the motor, or walked with me, I felt how honoured I was to be his mother, he was so splendid and so modest and delightful, and he loved no company so much as that of his own folk. He dearly loved his home. I never knew anyone readier than he for Heaven. I can well imagine him there with his sweet smile, his strength and gentleness. The loss to me and to the neighbourhood is inexpressible, and yet, do you know, my mind is just filled with lovely pictures of his life, and with a great and glorious certainty that the day when I see Laurence again with Jesus will make up for all the tears and sorrows."

Oliver wrote from Mesopotamia : " He was the best of brothers. His life was an example to me of Christianity put into practice, and I pray God that He may give me grace to reflect the love of Christ in my own life as Laurence did in his. His religion, though not often on his lips, was always in his heart and visible in his face. His death, too, is an inspiration, for he fell both as a soldier of King Jesus and a soldier of the earthly King, and I pray God that when I cross the river, be it early or late, I may face death with the same high courage and simple faith."

Far back in her girlhood Mary used to have many thoughts of the Unseen World. In Dr. Glasgow's last year on earth (1890) she wrote : " Grandpapa has been talking to me a great deal lately about Heaven. I can never bring myself to think out any definite idea of Heaven; my conclusion always is, ' Eye hath not seen nor ear heard '; but I love to hear someone else talk about it. Grandpapa always speaks of it with such emotion, it makes a thrill go through you." What were her thoughts of Heaven now, amid ' the sufferings of this present time? ' To her and many another mother the Great War seemed to give a new power of vision, enabling them to look beyond the dark things of earth and *see* the life of Heaven. " Our Laurence," she wrote, " is now in one of the heavenly armies of pure spirits who follow the Lamb whithersoever He goeth. With what joy he now follows Jesus to victory ! "

Alan David Brown was born at Agharainy on September 22, 1907, and from the first, as we learn from the *Manuscript,* he was not quite so robust as his brothers had been. He was nursed by Mrs. Gleeson, who has been for many years not so much a faithful servant as a good friend of the family. " I was afraid," she says, " that his mother might be hurt when the little one refused, as sometimes happened, to go even to her. But on these occasions she would merely smile and say, ' Mother's time will come later on.' "

Being from his infancy kept as much as possible out of doors, Alan became, as the MS. says, " a great open-air boy." He was not precociously fond of books, even of picture-books, but he became exceedingly deft with his hands. Oliver was clever at mechanics, and Alan would sit for hours and watch him making things; then he would try to make them himself. In his seventh year, during the Easter holidays, he watched and, as far as little hands could, eagerly assisted his brothers, who were building a house in the garden by their own labour—laying the bricks and mortar, covering the timber roof with thatch, putting in the door and windows. The little house, fourteen feet long by eight wide, was well and truly built, and may stand as long as Agharainy itself. On the last Christmas which brought all the five children together (1914), they cooked their dinner there, and had plenty of fun over it, as one can imagine.

As the faithful MS. records, Alan was " slow of

ALAN WITH HIS SISTERS.

learning to read." Not till he was nine was he "just beginning to read to himself for his own pleasure. His first start off was with *Robin Hood,* a nice little edition for children, easy to hold." He never willingly missed his Aunt Ada's class in the Castlecaulfield Sunday School. Learning very early to cycle, he rode daily to the Royal School in Dungannon. Alike at home and school, he threw himself into games with astonishing energy. At his mother's invitation a number of schoolboys of about his own age came out to Agharainy every Saturday morning, and Alan, the cleverest of all with his fingers, took delight in preparing ploys for them and initiating them into some of the crafts which he was already learning. When the head-master of the Royal School gave prizes for "Handiworks," Alan was first in his class.

From his own and his mother's letters to the trenches of France and the plains of Mesopotamia we gather what pleasant—no, the right word is "jolly"—Saturday mornings all the boys spent at Agharainy. Now we see them weaving baskets with willow branches cut from the orchard trees—"some of them not badly," Alan judges; now they make dainty little houses with the pith of elder boughs; now they play French card-games and do paper folding, the latter as a lesson in neatness and exactness. One morning "Catch-my-Pal" (Rev. R. J. Patterson) drops in upon them and gives them a great time, sending them afterwards cards with the design of a Y.M.C.A. Hut, to be cut out and folded and set up. Another day each

boy draws a Lighthouse, while Alan's mother teaches
them all to sing—

> Comme une phare sur la plage,
> Perçant l'ombre de la nuit,
> L'amour de Dieu dans l'orage
> Guide l'homme et le conduit.*

" My little class," she wrote, " goes on merrily.
They all enjoy it very much, and so do I." With
tasks and games, stories and songs, the morning hours
go swiftly past, and " we wind up with an apple to
help them on their homeward way."

Alan's two last letters, written on Sunday afternoons
in the early spring of 1918 and sent out to Mesopotamia, throb with the vital energy of an eager boyish
spirit. If he does not spell or punctuate quite so well
as some boys of ten, be it noted that his French was
quite as good as his English. " I have just been
doing my Bible study," he says in the first letter.
" Mother is reading a lovly book called *The
Schonberg Cotta Family* perhaps you have herd of it
before On Saterday we had a kind of paper-chase
when the boys came we first sung our French hymne
and played the French game and then mother expained
what they were to do in French then we went out and
gathered a lot of larel leaves Then Pollock and I
went of and we got 6 minutes start about half way we

* One may translate :
> Like a high and flashing light,
> Flung across the stormy sea,
> Love Divine in darkest night
> Safely guideth you and me.

had no more leaves It was great fun . . . All
the Wolf-cubs had a Church parade at Mr. Sides's
Church* and they intend to come to our Church some
day."

Alan's letter of the following Sunday is written in still
higher spirits, and even a wire sent by his big brother
with the best of tidings from Mesopotamia is for the
moment forgotten in the joy of a splendid home victory
which must be announced. " There are great rejicings
at school now yesterday we won the Medallion we
beat Methody 16 to nil the two boys who scored
were Steel and Nixon the boys brought down two
chairs to the station and then carried the two boys
round the town. They had a Concert afterwards and
eatch one had to do something. . . . We were
glad to get the telegram to say that you were better."
The message which had been wired was, " Quite well
—convalescent—Amara." This meant that after being
in a fever hospital at Bagdad, Oliver had been able
to go into the Convalescent Camp at Amara, on the
Tigris.

Alan was just ten when Laurence fell at Ypres—old
enough to feel the pang of a great personal sorrow.
In mind and spirit he was developing rapidly. As his
mother wrote, " He was more and more getting to be
a delightful companion, sensible and interesting, so
pleasant and bright, as well as good and kind and
thoughtful." She tells how often she was cheered by
his singing and whistling about the house. " Youthful
spirits rise, notwithstanding sorrow which is very real.

* The Church of Ireland, Castlecaulfield.

It is a mercy. Children in the house and plenty of work to do are the best cures for depressed thoughts, next of course to faith in God."

All through the winter Alan appeared to be in good health. But when the primroses and the swallows came, the bloom faded from his cheeks, and the specialist who was summoned from Belfast found that he was suffering from an obscure form of anæmia, for which no cure has yet been discovered.

His illness, lasting two months, was, in his mother's pathetic words, "a long-drawn-out distress," during which "he was always uncomplaining." She read French and English books of adventure to him. After finishing the three volumes of Jules Verne's *Les Enfants du Capitaine Grant,* they turned to *Robinson Crusoe,* not, as at a previous reading, an abbreviated edition, but the complete book. Sometimes he played a game of draughts. One morning seven or eight aeroplanes flew over the house, and his little bed was turned round so that he might see them out of the window. He was greatly interested; as mother had just been reading to him, in the *Children's Magazine,* about the history of aeroplanes, it was wonderfully appropriate. Another day he revealed what lay very near his heart by wistfully asking, "Do you think the boys will come on Saturday?"

Happily he slept much, and in his waking hours he was always cheerful. "He was a brave little soldier of Christ," his mother wrote to Oliver, feeling that he merited the words of praise as much as any lad who went gallantly over the parapet.

On a June evening she sat beside him preparing for *Woman's Work* the papers she had received in the morning regarding the annual meetings in Belfast. For Alan there was no valley or river, and no sadness of farewell. " I think I'm going to Church, Gleeson," he said, as he gently sank to sleep. Then his breath failed. The youngest of the Agharainy family had gone to be with the eldest in the land where sorrow is unknown.

" I had no idea," wrote his mother, " how near was the end. Nor had he. It would be a glad surprise to find himself in the Better Land with Jesus, with Laurence, perfectly blessed and happy. It all seems like a dream—to think of our wee son, Alan, who seemed so safe compared to the other two. Ah, it is hard to part with that darling. I need not begin to say how dear he was. How rich I was with five, and now only three. But I must not say *only*. We are rich still. They are all so dear. God is testing our faith. He is willing to show His power and His love in strengthening us to stand. We are getting a lot of letters, some very touching ones from Sunday School children and from Alan's school-fellows. We stay ourselves on the Rock of Ages."

Just before the outbreak of the war Mary had begun to use Canon Harford-Battersby's little book called *DAILY, a Help to Private Prayer,* on the blank pages of which are to be entered, with the dates, " Special Subjects for Prayer," while on the opposite pages, also with the dates, are to be set down " Answers to Prayer." Her last subject but one in the book is dated

April 21, 1918, and is simply a petition "For Alan."
Opposite this, under the date June 7, stand two
Answers : "Nevertheless, not my will but Thine be
done." "To depart and to be with Christ, which is
far better."

Three days later she wrote to Oliver : "Alan's sweet
bright spirit has fled back to God—his true home.
Sometimes I think that this is worse than Laurence's
going. At least I had given up Laurence long before,
and his life, though short, seemed so complete in a way,
while Alan was just a little way started on his journey.
But God knows best. Alan served him faithfully, too,
and leaves a bright and sweet memory, fragrant of
goodness and kindness and love. Ah, dear, such as he
are so much needed. How many things are dark. We
must walk by faith, holding on tightly to God's hand
in the dark, confident that all is right."

A week later she wrote to Oliver again, now from
Downing's Bay in County Donegal, whither she went
for a brief rest. "As I go about this lovely spot, I
keep thinking how much more lovely is the country
which Alan and Laurence inhabit. I have often
pictured myself being called away and leaving all you
dear five. I knew I should not dread to do so; you
were all on the right, the safe road; and I have had
such a happy life, and had such a glorious prospect,
that I could go with joy. But I never contemplated
two being called away before. It is as well we do
not know beforehand. God is love, and we can trust
Him to do right." Then her mind reverts to Nature
and its teaching, as if the austere beauty of a Donegal

coast were somehow like the judgment and mercy of God. " The lights and shadows and gleams of sunshine are lovely." And when her mother-heart still ached, now for Laurence and now for Alan, she found consolation in the thoughts expressed in one of R. L. Stevenson's poems :

Yet, O stricken heart, remember, O remember,
　How of human days he lived the better part;
April came to bloom, and never dim December
　Breathed its killing chills upon the head or heart.

Doomed to know not Winter, only Spring, a Being
　Trod the flowery April blithely for a while,
Took his fill of music, joy of thought and seeing,
　Came and stayed and went, nor ever ceased to smile.

Came and stayed and went, and now when all is
　　finished,
　You alone have crossed the melancholy stream,
Yours the pang, but his, O his the undiminished,
　Undecaying gladness, undeparted dream.

All that life contains of torture, toil and treason,
　Shame, dishonour, death to him were but a name,
Here, a boy, he dwelt through all the singing season,
　And ere the day of sorrow, departed as he came.

CHAPTER VIII

THE CROWN OF LIFE

THE Special Subjects set down in Mary's *DAILY, a Help to Private Prayer,* are a sure index to her deepest thoughts. Extending over a period of five years, which include the four of the war, they are of far more than private interest. They reveal not only the tender heart of a suffering mother, but what the Puritans called a public soul, inspired by the great hope of the speedy coming of Christ's Kingdom upon the earth.

Some of the brief petitions naturally give touching expression to hopes and fears for two brave soldier boys. "June 29, 1916: That Laurence may get safe home to-morrow; for a blessing to all on his time at home. For Oliver, that he may soon get home." Opposite the first half is written on July 25, "Abundantly answered. A very happy visit. Returned this day to Aldershot." And the Answer to the second part appears on Nov. 6, "Oliver home after two months in St. Thomas' Hospital. Well and bright." "God bless the lads," is one of the oldest of all prayers, which will be daily repeated so long as the young and daring go out into the world to face danger and death. And believing prayer does not cease though the answer may widely differ from what has been fondly hoped for. Twelve days after Laurence's death at Ypres there is entered (Aug. 28, 1917) the Special Prayer, " For a blessing on any card or leaflet about my darling Laur," and opposite this, on Jan. 28, 1918, appears the Answer, which knocks strangely at the heart, " Everybody likes the booklet about Laurence; preached on, given to Sunday School. Bless the Lord, O my soul."

The little Prayer-book also proves that special requests were daily uttered or silently breathed for Country and Empire. Opposite the Prayer of three words, "God save Ireland " (April 7, 1914) stands the glad Answer of Aug. 14, shadowed by a sentence in brackets, " Unionists and Nationalists unite against a common enemy. (Seen later that union is only apparent)." A glorious hope in the first days of the war, followed by a sore disappointment ! Some comfort is sought in yet another addition, " But Ireland is peaceful, H(ome) R(ule) does not seem at all likely." That peace, too, proved illusory, being only the lull before the storm of the following Easter. But the patriotic Prayer will be answered in God's good time. His " salvation " is grander than any political term.

On Sep. 15, 1915, two Prayers are entered together, " For Victory : For Prohibition "—boons evidently associated very closely in the writer's mind, as in America's and Canada's, but, alas ! not yet in Britannia's. . . . On May 28, 1916, Mary enters this four-fold Special Prayer for daily use :

" That the war may soon be ended. That a righteous peace may be established. That the enemy may come to a right mind. For Revival of Religion in our own land." Opposite these petitions, which expressed the deepest longings of her heart, there are no answers, only a white page as it were patiently waiting for them. The writer lived to see the answer to the first, but not to record it. . . . In May 1917, stands the two-fold petition, " That victory may soon be given in Palestine and Syria, and famine relieved." On the opposite side are the Answers : " Dec. 1917, Jerusalem taken and further progress " ; " June 1918, £700 given for Palestine Relief in response to a letter in the press by Rev. Edward Clarke."*

It is significant that one Special Subject appears in *DAILY* much more frequently than any other, and that the last, entered on May 3, 1918, is in the four words, " For July W. W." The capitals mean, of course, *Woman's Work*. No number of the Magazine was ever prepared and issued without the most earnest thought and prayer. On Dec. 14, 1914, we find the petition, " That January W. W. may be quite right and for the glory of Christ and the progress of His Kingdom. That circulation may be doubled." Opposite this, on June 15, 1915, is the joyous Answer, " Circulation is doubled." . . . On May 20, 1915, " For July W. W., that it may be much used of God—free from mistakes. That circulation may go up to 40,000. For a great blessing on

*Minister of Strabane, Convener of Jewish Committee.

THE EDITOR.

the circulars sent out to-day." There is another blank
on the opposite page, indicating a devout hope not yet
realised. But who can doubt that the Church will see
this prayer of the Editor answered—will indeed answer
it? . . . On July 30, 1915, "For October W. W.,
that suitable material may come in and in good time.
That it may speak for God." Answer on September 10, "Quite too much material, and good, and in
good time."

The sudden doubling of the readers of the Magazine
in the second year of the War was a very striking and
gratifying fact. Before 1914 the circulation, which
was only 7,000 when Mary became Editor, had crept up
to 13,500 copies, and this was considered by many very
creditable. But when Mrs. Brown reached her twenty-
fifth year of office, her husband, who was always heart
and soul with her in any forward movement, resolved to
celebrate the event by having the Magazine enlarged and
illustrated in colour. At the same time an effort was
made to get a copy taken by every household in the
Church, and the success which crowned the effort was
largely due to the newly-formed Girls' Auxiliary, whose
zeal, Mary felt, was a prophecy of greater things in the
near future. To carry all this through in war-time was
a notable achievement. "Few can realise," as Mrs.
Fred. O'Neill says, "the time devoted to this under-
taking by these two enthusiastic workers. God
blessed them in it, and the circulation of *Woman's
Work* reached its high water mark, while our Church
possessed the unique distinction of having the only
missionary magazine in the world illustrated throughout in colour."

N

A letter of the Editor to a friend expresses her aspirations at that time. " I am so glad you like *Woman's Work* in its new form. It is appealing to a lot of people who formerly never looked at a missionary magazine. I think it is only right that missionary and religious literature should have as attractive an appearance as any other. Last winter, when we feared for Missions at the outbreak of War, the word came to me, ' What is that in thy hand? ' and I felt sure that God called me to develop and use to the utmost this little magazine which is so big a part of my life. I thank and praise him for the blessing granted. I do want it to be a power for the spiritual life of our Church. . . . I am very anxious that many should follow out the Bible study. Too many are content with detached passages when their spiritual life needs the whole Word of God. It is because thorough Bible Study is so much needed, and I see the possibility of enthusiastic work at it, that I am *very* anxious to know of many going in for it."

An editorial article headed " After Twenty-Five Years " (*Woman's Work*, January, 1915), also helped to increase the circulation. It could not but go straight to the reader's heart. " I appeal," the Editor says, " to every woman and girl in the Church to do her part. When we get that accomplished, shall we have done a small thing? Can we say it is small when we remember that such missionaries as Hudson, Livingstone, Martyn, and Marsden were all led to the Mission Field through the reading of missionary literature? This thought makes me certainly thank God for the work He has put into my hands. If only

Woman's Work can help others to go out, how richly rewarded all we who are helping together with it shall be. Some of us wanted to go to ' the regions beyond ' and were not allowed to go, but for each and all of us there is much to do. We can, by the grace of God, help those at home to realise that the only thing worth living for is to do all the will of God, and we know that His will is THAT ALL MEN SHOULD BE SAVED. For this great and wonderful work, He uses weak, human instruments, if only they yield themselves to Him. What an honour is ours to be fellow-workers with Him ! "

The Editorial of a year later (January, 1916) is entitled " Let us thank God and take Courage." It is full of interesting matter, and the last sentences are singularly impressive. " A year ago *Woman's Work* had twenty-four pages and no coloured pictures, now it has thirty-six pages and brightness and colour such as young people, and many old ones too, delight in. We think our Church has reason to be proud of what Irish artists and Irish printers have produced. And we have good reason to believe that for every one who read each copy of our magazine in former days three or four are reading it now. Our missionaries' letters, so vivid and heart-stirring, written often with great difficulty in the midst of their many occupations, are penetrating into all but a few of our congregations. What may we not hope for when so many more are praying for them and for their work? For we depend on our readers using the missionary magazine as a prayer manual. Through prayer only can we become ' mighty towards God to the pulling down of strongholds,' and the building up of the Church of Christ."

How the idea of coloured pictures took shape in her mind is worth recording. To one of the Indian Zenana workers she wrote : " God's world is full of beauty, colour and glory of all sorts, if we do not spoil it. We malign Him if we represent religion as dull and uninteresting. I have often felt that India is so wonderful in its animal life, its colouring of skies and garments and complexions, that the indistinct photos which generally adorn missionary publications must give a poor idea of the reality." The thought of reproducing these colours of the East appealed most strongly to her artistic instinct. An original idea captured her imagination and had to be realised. Her husband and she had chanced to learn that when the American *Geographic Magazine* began to give its readers beautiful illustrations, often in colours, its circulation ere long increased twenty-fold. " We thought," writes Mr. Brown, " if the people who are interested in geography appreciate the best, why should not those who are interested in Missions do so also? We found that they do, and that an immense field is thus open to missionary agencies, if they will follow the lead and combine to produce the best and most attractive literature."

It was Mary's cherished dream that all the missionary societies would ere long unite in asking their most gifted writers and colour-artists to provide missionary literature for common use in their respective magazines; that they would one and all adopt a standard magazine page, so that the cost of the finest production would be greatly diminished, one central printing-place working for all alike; that the big missionary societies, such as the C.M.S., would in this way render a vast service by co-operating with the smaller; and that each missionary magazine, while true to its own cause, would at the same time inspire its readers with the missionary enthusiasm of the Church Universal, and do its part in uniting all the fighting forces of Christ's Kingdom for the spiritual conquest of the world. All this was no mere passing thought in Mary's mind, but an end which she kept in view during years of strenuous labour, always with a single desire to give an uplift to the whole missionary journalism of the world.

On April 7, 1914, this Special Prayer is set down in *DAILY*: "For the Foreign Languages Scheme, R.S.D. [Royal School, Dungannon] that it may be thoroughly successful, and that it may be for the glory of God." Opposite this, on August 8, the Answer is thankfully recorded: " Girls' trip truly successful. Boys' First Camp also. Second Camp only got as far as Paris. Got home safe and happy." Behind all this there lies a very great amount of thought and labour. As we read in the *Manuscript*: " All through the years 1913 and 1914 I was very busy corresponding about Foreign Travel Schemes. In June, 1914, I accompanied Miss MacDermott and her pupils to Ste. Croix and Chaux-de-fonds. Alice and Dorothy came, too, and we had a happy time. I felt nervous about it a bit beforehand, feeling the responsibility of taking charge of so many girls. We were a party of twenty-six. I quite lost all nervousness and felt the truth of this, ' Thou wilt keep him in perfect peace whose mind

is stayed on Thee, because he trusteth in Thee.' . .
The first we heard of war was on the last Sunday of
July, at Ste. Croix, when it was announced that
Austria had declared war on Serbia. Everyone said,
' This will mean a big European war.' We could not
realise what that meant, and we got peacefully home
on the last day of July. Two days later would have
meant great difficulty in Paris, where the men would
by that time have been mobilised.''

Miss Margaret V. M'Caughan, one of the teachers
who accompanied the Dungannon girls to Switzerland,
recalls a happiness which was shared by every member
of the party. '' I remember that trip abroad very
vividly. We had a châlet at Les Rasses, two miles
from Ste. Croix, on a lonely mountain road, opposite
the highest peak of the Juras. The things which
impressed me most in our leader, Mrs. Brown, were :
her calmness of mind, which never fussed or worried
while she was piloting twenty-six people through a
difficult journey; her unceasing thought for her
missionary friends—she was always reading letters
from them or writing to them; her love of her own
children, and her tireless thought for the children of
the party. . . . Though she did not dance herself, she liked us to do so. She had the most ingenious
games and competitions for wet days, and special
games for Sunday. . . . She had a knack of
taking the right way with the girls. She wanted them
to talk French always. They, of course, wanted to
talk English. She never scolded them if they talked
English, but always answered them in French, so that
gradually they came to use French naturally. . . .

She never went out without a pencil and paper, and when it was fine she went with us to the mountains. She was always sketching a tree, flower, or châlet. She had a remarkably strong nerve for a woman. She would go along giddy precipices calmly and without fear. I was never so impressed by her quiet mind as on those expeditions. . . . The girls loved her. She allowed them a remarkable amount of liberty, and none of them ever abused it. I know for a fact that some of them are trying to follow in her footsteps. I only wish she could know it too. Perhaps she does. I used to delight when she gave me some difficult thing to do. I would have gone through fire and water for her. I also remember her saying to me, when I commented on the fact that the arrangements went so smoothly, ' You know there is a great deal of prayer behind this trip. It has been prayed for ever since February.' "

Another member of the party says that none of those who formed it will ever forget the quiet Sunday afternoons, when their leader, with all the girls sitting round her on the grass of the mountain side, talked to them in the silence about the Gospel of Luke, making everything in the Life of Lives so real and vivid that the third Gospel was felt to be, what it has been well called, the most beautiful book in the world. At morning prayers a daily portion of it was read aloud by the girls themselves, each using a little French edition which she had presented to them. Probably none of the circle of listeners ever felt nearer the Kingdom of Heaven than they did in those Sabbath hours on the mount, and a passing angel, desiring to look into uncommon things, might have seen

.   .   .   .   beautiful and holy faces,
Lit with their loving and aflame with God.

But faith working by love makes the heavenliest things common everywhere, and the leader of the party in that quiet retreat had the strong conviction that in such gloriously simple ways the Christian girls of Ireland could bring back to their homeland a golden age.

Hélène Wehrlin also came to Ste. Croix to be with Mary, and she writes a touching note regarding her last meeting, as it proved, with her friend. "I had an invitation to go to Brussels," she says, "but something prompted me to go to Mary for a few days first. On July 22 I left Paris, and next afternoon I arrived at Les Rasses, where I found my old friend who was always the same. She was surrounded by a troop of young girls, whom she directed admirably. She had a special gift for keeping them happily employed, and in the evening she would play without ceasing the airs of Sir Roger de Coverley while they all enjoyed their sports. . . . But the hour was grave, very grave. On Sunday, July 26, when we were at our midday meal, a loud ring came at the door, and a domestic brought in a printed leaflet, the same as was being sent to all the chalets. It was an announcement of the ultimatum to Serbia. Then followed the feverish waiting for events. Two days later, in the morning of July 28, I said good-bye to Mary, who was next day to begin her own return journey with all her young band. Henceforward she and I were again to lead our lives apart, but none the less united, for were we not both pressing towards the end which is that of every servant of the Master? During the four days spent on that height I had many opportunities of being alone with my friend, and it was up there on the mountain that we saw each other for the last time.''

Foreign Languages Tours were also arranged for Dungannon schoolboys, and carried out under the direction of the head-master. In this scheme Mary had her husband's hearty co-operation. He remembered his own school holidays as wasted opportunities, weeks spent aimlessly at seaside resorts, when, had anyone thought of this plan, he might have been acquiring two or three foreign languages and storing his mind with memories of other lands and peoples. Whereas he had given a great deal of time to French and German, and yet in later life derived scarcely any benefit from them, his sons spoke them as living languages, and he knew that such a mastery was of inestimable value from every point of view.

One of the Dungannon schoolboys, who spent what he recalls as '' a glorious month '' in the Vosges with twenty Irish comrades and a hundred Paris Scouts (*Eclaireurs*), writes thus: '' Mrs. Brown's interest in the Royal School won for her a very warm place in our hearts. To her and her husband is due the success with which tours to the Continent were arranged for schoolboys engaged in the study of modern languages. Two of these had been most successfully carried through when the War broke out, and schemes of the kind had perforce to be suspended.

All my life I shall look back with pleasure on the happy days I spent in camp on the summit of Haut Jacques, above St. Dïë, a peaceful town since devastated by war. And in connection with these memories of sunny Eastern France I shall always think with gratitude of Mrs. Brown.''

One of the last themes in Mary's little book of Special Prayers had long engaged her attention. '' January 20, 1918 : For Alice's Sunday School class. For the propagation of Teacher Training plan.'' While supervising the work of her girl assistants in the Sunday School at Castlecaulfield, Mary had seen how great a help and encouragement it was to all young teachers to have the lesson gone over and explained to them beforehand. Moreover her mind had long been exercised by this problem : how to make the happiest use of the one short hour, on a Sunday morning or afternoon, which is all that is allowed to the Sunday School teacher, so pitifully short in comparison with the five days a week given to the teacher of secular sub-jects. She had always taken the duties of the Sunday School teacher very seriously, feeling, as she said, that it would be '' terrible '' to go and talk to a class with-out preparation. '' In the teaching of my own children and in Sunday School teaching,'' she reflects, '' I have always felt it the greatest incentive to careful prepara-tion and to the gathering of the brightest and best helps I could manage, that perchance I might, by my dull way of presenting the Bible, make it appear unin-teresting. It would be one of the greatest injuries I could do my dear children if I dulled or tarnished that bright jewel—the Word of God."

She was keenly alive to the fact that it would be deemed unfair to lay heavy responsibilities on untrained workers in any other position than that of Sunday School teaching, and she came to realise not only the great benefit, but the absolute necessity of giving young teachers some instruction in the best ways of interesting children and imparting the truth to their minds. In a letter to her son Oliver she describes her own simple but effective method. " After the children are dismissed I keep the young teachers for fifteen minutes and have a talk with them about the art of teaching and the magnitude of the work. I show them how necessary it is to have a ' point of contact ' to begin the lesson, something in the child's own life and experience leading up to it. Then I go over an outline of the lesson for next week, and we wind up with prayer. Each time I give the teachers a text for themselves—such as ' Lovest thou me? ' in the last chapter of John, and ' They that be wise shall shine, etc.,' in the end of Daniel. If you look at this last in a reference Bible you will see that for *wise* the margin gives *teachers*—' Those who are teachers, etc.' —a good text for teachers."

In both France and Ireland Mary had been rewarded as a teacher by seeing many definite decisions to follow Christ. Sometimes a letter would tell her that " the great transaction " was done, oftener she divined the truth from the new manner and spirit of a pupil. In her *DAILY* she prays " For all my S. S. Scholars, that each one may be a child of God, not one missing." She encouraged all young teachers to look with confidence for the Divine blessing on their work, yet she bade them not be disappointed if they had to wait. Truth is a germ which, once implanted in the mind, will by God's blessing blossom into beauty and yield abundant fruit, but growth cannot be forced. One soweth and another reapeth. Using another homely figure, she writes : " One person lays a fire carefully and well, another applies the match. It looks as if the latter lit the fire. But the match alone would have done nothing. It required the previous preparation. Both were needful."

There was another result, in Mary's estimation desirable beyond all others, which she expected from the Teachers' Training movement. An article entitled " A Talk on Sabbath School Teaching " (*Woman's Work,* Jan. 1917) ends with two sentences which are italicised by her to call the reader's attention to their importance. " Some will ask why should a method of Sabbath School teaching be described in a Missionary Magazine? *The Sabbath School is perhaps the earliest and most valuable training ground for our future missionaries. When you train young teachers, you are very possibly training missionaries.*"

On going to Belfast in the autumn of 1918, Mary had the happiness of being invited by her brother James, who is Superintendent of Windsor Church Sunday School, to take up again the work she had laid down there about a quarter of a century before. This gave her the opportunity of introducing, just as she had done at home, the new methods of grading pupils and helping young teachers. " It was owing to her enthusiasm and example," writes an experienced teacher, " that the Primary Departments in Windsor and Fisherwick were organised.   She took much trouble to inaugurate them personally, and evinced the greatest interest in their progress. It was her great desire to see the methods of the Graded Sunday School adopted all over the Church, and she looked forward to a winter in Belfast as affording her opportunities for helping to establish Primary Departments in many Sunday Schools."

One other entry in Mary's *Help to Private Prayer* somehow calls to mind St. Paul's words about " the care of all the Churches," as well as our Lord's wonderful sayings about " other sheep," " one flock," and " one Shepherd." It furnishes the last and most impressive evidence of the catholicity of the writer's sympathies. It was made on October 29, 1917, after the receipt of a letter from Dr. Margaret M'Neill of Kuanchangtzu, and it runs thus : " For Kao-cheng-en, teacher in Manchuria Arts College. For Pastor Kung. For Pastor Chu of Newchwang. For Elder Chang of Fakumen." If ever this Memoir should fall into the hands of that teacher, those pastors, and that elder, they will be surprised, and probably not a little awed, to learn that their names have been found in the book of the Private Devotions of an Irish saint.

The fact is infinitely suggestive, and indicates the most hopeful line of human progress. The spiritual future of our race, which is its real future, will probably be determined far more largely by woman than man. For sixteen hundred years a Christendom of fighting men has notoriously and ignominiously failed to convince a sceptical world that all lands and peoples are one in Christ Jesus. In five years of our era Christian brotherhood has been proved by the slaughter of ten million brothers. Are God's resources, then, exhausted? No, the world has yet to learn, be it very reverently said, what can be done for it by a Christendom of praying women. Queen Mary of Scotland confessed that she dreaded one man's prayers more than an army of twenty thousand men. She did not know that by using the same means she could have wielded the same power. The truth is at last known; praying woman has Omnipotent Love on her side; and the world may await the result with perfect confidence. "O woman, great is thy faith : be it unto thee as thou wilt."

In the autumn of 1918 it was decided to close Agharainy for the winter, Mrs. Brown going with Alice and Honor to reside at Mount Randal. Towards the end of August, just before leaving home, she wrote a touching letter which reveals where her heart still was. "The 16th was our silver wedding day, also the anniversary of Laurence's departure. We made no fuss about it. Our dear ones are safe with God, and we are in His loving care as well as they. We must keep looking up, having our 'conversation' in Heaven. . . . I constantly seem to see Laur beside me, smiling his kind, bright smile and saying, 'Don't fret, mother, God makes all things work

together for good.' It was his firm faith. Alan's
dear image and his are always with me. I miss Alan
more, not less, as the days go by. Two sons have
we in Heaven now—truly Heaven grows to be more
and more our real home. Often it seems to me that
those two sweet boys are not far away—I think they
must be ministering spirits."

Going to Belfast in the beginning of September,
Mary spent two busy and quickly passing months
there. Those were the thrilling days of the allied
advance, when every hour brought victory nearer.
They were also, alas! the depressing days in which
Europe felt the grip of a virulent influenza whose
victims were numbered by millions. During all that time
f mingled hope and fear Mary had her hand in God's
ind her heart at rest. Being very patriotic, she watched
.he closing act of the tremendous world-drama with
fervent gratitude to God, while her personal sorrows
never drew from her lips a murmuring word. It was
commonly remarked that she seemed to be sustained
by an unexhausted reserve of spiritual elation and
enthusiasm. " I met her one day in town," says a
young friend of hers, " though she did not see me, and
she went past me with her face shining."

Having heard from Oliver that he was planning a
visit to some of the Mission stations in Gujarat and
Kathiawar, she wrote to him on October 8 : " I often
have day dreams—for instance, of aeroplanes becom-
ing fairly common after the war and safe as motors.
You would, I fancy, learn to ride one. Fancy taking
Alice (she has the adventurous spirit) and visiting the
Mission stations in Manchuria ! I have heard Dr.

Elizabeth Beatty say she would like an aeroplane to carry her over the awful Chinese roads."

Next week (October 15) she wrote Oliver a letter which shows her jubilant over the political emancipation of women, and earnestly grappling with the problem of "getting them enlightened as to the possibilities of their vote. People here do not half know what has been accomplished in Canada and the United States."

Her letter to her son written on the following Tuesday (October 22) has her golden word "Missions" used seven times like a refrain. Part of it is as follows : "Yesterday, by request, I went to the Ladies' Zenana Meeting at Rosemary Street to talk to them, and among other things they were interested to hear what I quoted from your letter about the lectures by Missionaries and various efforts to interest the soldiers in Missions. So you see you are helping. All you say about your studies in Hindustani is most interesting. You do well to learn it and as much about the country as you can. As you say, the knowledge will be most useful to you in whatever path of life God leads you. Alice and Honor are plunged into work for Missions here. . . Next Saturday afternoon the Girls' Auxiliary is to have an ' At Home ' in the Lecture Hall. They work for the soldiers as well as for Missions."

On the following Friday, with her love of music as strong as ever, Mary went to the Ulster Hall and heard the Philharmonic Choir render Bach's motet, " Be not Afraid," and the part song, " God gives the Night." Next Tuesday (October 29) she wrote a letter so characteristic that her friends who read it will seem to

hear her voice. It is the message of a vigilant intellect
au courant of all public affairs, a tender heart rooted
in simple mother-love, a prayerful spirit reposing on
the unchanging love of God. " We are so happy these
days," she says to Oliver, " in the thought that the
end of war draws near. To-day we have news of
Austria's accepting President Wilson's demands. It is
grand how Palestine and Syria are being cleared of the
Turk. I wonder what they will set you to next. Helping to restore peace and good government will be
happy, happy work. Father is very anxious to get
some ladies into Parliament to go for Temperance and
other Reform. We think Cousin X. would be good
for it, but she does not care for the idea. . . .
The girls are busy at school. Yesterday Honor was
playing lacrosse for the first time and liked it very
much. They go in for that at Miss Nairn's. God
bless you, dearest boy, and bring you soon safe home
again. Your loving Mother." Then she laid down
her pen for ever.

She went the same afternoon to the annual Conference of the Ulster Temperance Council, at which her
husband was chairman, and heard a well-known
American lecturer, Dr. G. A. Henry, use the words :
" The Ulster Temperance Council is much like the
American Anti-Saloon League—an organisation whose
final fruitage will be total Prohibition for your beautiful
Island." To this prophecy she doubtless said Amen,
for all through the war the subject had been con-
stantly in her thoughts and prayers. She knew that the
American temperance victory had been achieved by
American women, and she had dreams of enfranchised

o

British women smiting the giant evil in the United Kingdom and not needing to strike twice. It was her last public meeting.

On that October evening she caught a chill, and next day she was not able to go out. No danger was apprehended for some time, but on the following Sunday the doctors found the presence of pneumonia, and next day she was critically ill. As the days passed she remained conscious, though now and then her mind seemed to wander. She talked of *Woman's Work* practically the whole time, usually in English, sometimes in French. She feared she would not be able to have the January number ready in time. Just before she became ill she had received a beautiful series of coloured photographs illustrating Mission work in heathen lands. These were put on the mantelpiece where she could see them, and her troubled mind became peaceful as her eyes gazed at them. India, she decided, was to go in first, then Manchuria.

Sometimes she thought of the children. Had Alice done her practising? Had Honor finished her lessons? Public questions were sometimes on her mind, and she would half-consciously plead for temperance, or murmur sympathetic words about the privations of the prisoners of war. When she spoke of little Alan her face was angelic. "Her sweet and saintly patience" deeply moved the doctors who saw her daily.

She made a brave fight for life, and seemed confident that she would conquer. To a sister-in-law who visited her every day she said, "You *don't* think I am going to die? I do not want to leave them." And in her affectionate words to her husband there was no suggestion of farewell.

On Friday morning Mrs. Alek imagined she saw some improvement, and went back to Easthope, which is close to Mount Randal, to tell Mary's beloved eldest brother. "When I returned to Mount Randal," she says, " after a few minutes, Mr. Brown met me at the door, and said, ' She is gone.' Then Grannie (Lady Crawford) joined us and said, ' Yes, she is gone. Life will never be the same again. Mary was more than my daughter, she was the best friend I ever had.' "

The exceedingly simple funeral took place on Monday, November 11, a day which the world will never forget—the day of the Armistice. At eleven o'clock, just as the little procession passed down the Avenue of Mount Randal, the bells began to ring. Sir William Crawford, almost an octogenarian, was too feeble to accompany the funeral to Donaghmore. But he did an extraordinary thing. He did it simply, without thought, in obedience to some imperious instinct of patriotism and Christian faith. When he heard the bells he said, " It must be the Armistice. Go and call the gardeners and we will get the flag up." And by 11.30 the flag was waving on Mount Randal. Verily a strange thing! But Mary had given her son to have that flag flying, and the father who had known her heart so truly all those fifty years may well have felt that her spirit moved him to give that command.

* * * * * *

In the mystic light of memory, Mary lives for some of her friends as she was at the moment when her spirit first touched theirs, leaving an impression which time can never efface. One of them, who became a missionary in Gujarat, remembers a day long ago, when, as a little girl, Mary sang the beautiful French translation (by Theodore Monod) of one of the best-known Sankey hymns—

> Sur Toi, je me repose,
> O Jésu ! mon Sauveur.

" I can recall very vividly," says Miss Irwin, " the picture which impressed itself so strongly on all who were present that afternoon in the Castlerock Manse. The spiritual sweetness of the child's face seemed an appropriate setting for the words, with their suggestion of a rest and assurance not of this world."

Some of those who knew her all their days recall this or that surprising moment as most truly revealing her. Her second brother, James, says : "When I was beginning to earn some money, and had a little to spare, Mary said to me one day, ' Jemmy, what would you think of giving a pound to the Foreign Mission Collection? ' I may say I gasped. Such an idea had never entered my head. Nevertheless I did as was suggested, and never regretted doing so. A year or two later I told the incident to a young friend who was situated as I had been. He did not say much at the time, but afterwards he asked me if I remembered speaking to him of the matter. He told me he too had followed the suggestion and was glad he had done so."

Mary is remembered by her friends as one who

seemed always young. Even when she had reached middle life she retained a look and manner singularly girlish. She had the spirit of youth and it renewed itself day by day. In a letter to Hélène we find her philosophising very cheerfully on the flight of time, for once, it might appear, in the mood of Montaigne rather than of Pascal. " You say you are growing old. You will grow young again when you return here. I think one never grows old here. For my part I have not time to think of growing old. The years go by all the same, but I don't mind that (cela m' est égal). I should not like to be always young; it would become monotonous. I have never found that youth was so very free from cares. Looking back upon my life I find that until now it has always been bettering itself, always growing more and more happy, and I do not think it is merely outward circumstances which have brought that about. You see I am falling into philosophy, but it is you who draw me on in this way."

Her son Oliver alludes in a letter from the East to " Mother's perfect health." This may occasion some surprise, but it was essentially true. Her own letters prove how much attention she devoted to the subject of health, personal, domestic, national. She had been delicate in her girlhood, and could never expect to be very robust. Writing some time before her marriage she had humorously asked : " Would you like to know how ponderous I am? Hardly 7st 11lb. Last time I was weighed it was 8st 1lb." But in hygiene, as in other essential things, she was characteristically thorough, and by simply taking care she made herself capable of going through a very great amount of work without feeling fatigue. She loved all kinds of open-air exercise, such as walking, cycling, sea-bathing, and tennis; she had faith in the power of spirit over body; she studied diet scientifically, and became largely fruitarian in her meals. She had her reward, as many remarks in her letters indicate. " I really have excellent health, greatly improved by the system." "My health regimen, come to from experiences and experiments, is a good steadier of nerves." She was always grateful to the Providence that had taken her out of the city. " She once told me," says one of her missionary guests, " that the open-air treatment and sunshine of the country had built up her slightly fragile constitution into a much stronger one; that had she married and settled in Belfast she wouldn't have had half the health or full enjoyment of life which fell to her lot in Donaghmore."

One of Mary's friends rightly speaks of her as "amazingly simple." Some people found her perplexing, not having the key to a mind so original, a spirit so fine, a heart so deep. They were mystified by a character in which Hebrew austerity, Hellenic charm and Christian grace all met and blended. But little children, and all who had the spirit of little children, understood and loved her.

The note of austerity in her was very real. "Though she was very tender," writes Helen Waddell, " I can imagine her stern. If a thing were one's duty, it would have to be done. Not that she would force you to it. But there was a singleness of eye about her, a sheer incapacity of going any other way, that would shame you into doing it. I think she would have been relentless with herself. I believe her definition of life would have been the old Quaker one— to do the will of God."

Her doing of God's will was accompanied by a quiet acceptance of it in which her friends learned to imitate her. "When I heard that she was gone," says a young Indian missionary, " I could not take it in. I thought fiercely, God *couldn't* take her, she was doing such a great work for Him, which no one else can do. Then at once the words which she had quoted to me so often came into my heart—' That *good*, and *acceptable*, and *perfect* will of God.' I remember how slowly and distinctly she said this, and how she added, ' Think over each word,' and I know that her going from us is His perfect will."

Many qualities were combined in her most attractive grace—her genius for friendship. In one of her early letters to Hélène Wehrlin she wrote : " I have not the talent for showing the affection I feel, but it is there —the affection—and I think indeed that I have the gift of constancy." Her intuition told her that, like everybody else, she wanted " the show of affection as well as the affection itself." God Himself, she reasoned, wants both, and must be disappointed if we do not tell Him of our love. " The way He uses every relationship of life to illustrate His love to us makes us think so." She therefore set herself to correct a tendency to reserve which she saw as a fault in herself. And in later years we often find her letting herself go in language of affection like the following :

" Dear, I love you not less but more than at any time in the past. Any love or sympathy you get is no *drain* upon me. The heart grows by loving. ' The greatest of these is love.' I thank God for all the love in my lot, both giving and receiving."

Knowing so well her gift for friendship, she could smile if anyone doubted it. She was not " the cool and collected iceberg that some people thought " ; she wanted all the love she could get, and she could give " just about as much in return ! " Her dear friend Maude MacBride (now Mrs. Walker) once said to her long ago, "You're my Mont Blanc," and got the startling answer, " Mont Blanc with a volcano inside ! " And if evidence be wanted of her constancy, one has only to remember that she won three schoolgirl friends in Paris some forty years ago, one French, one Norwegian, and one Irish, and to-day the memory of her steadfast friendship is, one feels quite sure, their most sacred and cherished possession. To each of them she was to the end " *Ton amie toujours fidèle et dévouée.*"

Her genius for friendship took yet another and a higher form. She is remembered by all her friends as having the peculiar happiness of the mystic. That may seem the least definable of qualities, but she was always surprised if people saw anything strange in it. For her the mystic union between Christ and the soul was just essential Christianity. The Christian life, as she lived it, was a Divine service irradiated by a Divine friendship. That was her secret, which she was always trying to share with others, especially with the young. Her daughter Alice once asked what was her favourite hymn, and she answered that while there were many, both English and French, which were very dear to her, she thought the one she loved best was " Jesus, the very thought of Thee." In its original form—" Jesu, dulcis memoria "—this hymn comes from the heart of the great mystic, St. Bernard of Clairvaux.

In the most anxious period of the War that sacred friendship was Mary's all in all. " I think," she wrote in Feb. 1916, " I may say I am in love with Jesus Christ, and grow more and more so as I study the Gospels, Acts, and now Romans, to try and make them simple enough for the young. Pray especially for me now with Romans. I have read it over and over in A.V. and R.V., in the Weymouth N.T., in the 20th Century N.T., and in Conybeare and Howson. I have not yet finished it all in each of these, but parts in all and all in some. The result will, I hope, not be difficult, but very simple. The simple may be also very deep, and being God's word must be powerful."

The simple may be very deep! " Her own great simplicity," writes Helen Waddell, " she carried into every relation. She had no embarrassment in speaking of religion. She seemed to give herself away with both hands. And yet the last impression was of an impenetrable unconscious reserve. ' The misthress was someway remote in herself,' says an old servant in *The Soundless Tide:* it might have been spoken of her. I suppose it is true of all the mystics : their life is hid with Christ in God."

Probably Mary's missionary friends found it least difficult to read her inner mind, just because their dreams and visions were also hers. She was their Editor, and it was her labour of love to mediate between them and the Church at home. One of them might, in playful mood, address her as " My dear Woman's Work," as if she and " Maga " were one. But they all knew her as an Editor of an exceptional order, who gave to each of them and desired from each of them that beautiful friendship which is the finest fruit of Christian faith. The nearer the radii of a Christian circle come to the Centre, the nearer they come to one another. " For us missionaries in Manchuria," says Miss E. C. M'Mordie, " Mrs. Brown was the outstanding member of the Zenana Committee. We loved her, many of us, next to our own family circles. Her letters were something to look forward to, and to share with others, for she was the one we all knew." Writing from Anand in Gujarat, Mrs. R. H. Boyd says : " Every time I was with her it seemed natural to go on to think of Jesus ; and when I got one of her letters, so clearly and beautifully written, and so unhurriedly (though I knew the piles and piles of work she had to get through), I always felt as if she were talking to me, and I always got such a message that I read and re-read it and carried it about until I knew it by heart." So cordial and intimate, indeed, were Mary's relations with the Zenana workers that she came to think of them as more than friends. " No doubt could we have," says Miss Jane Beatty, who has laboured both in India and China, " that she was kept at home to do a great work for Missions. Once she said in my hearing, ' I have

never had a sister, but I look upon Zenana missionaries as my sisters.' "

Mary is remembered by all her friends as one who
deeply realised the mysteries of life and yet never
doubted the love of God. She had a thinker's mind,
which could not but ask questions and try to solve
enigmas. Even as a girl she found herself at home in
the deepest book of the Old Testament—the Book of
Job. "Do you know," she wrote as a young teacher
in Windsor, "I have liked to have Job to teach.
It gives the opportunity of speaking of the
reason and uses of trouble coming to the children of God. My girls were quite interested
when we found out about God as a Father, a Doctor,
a Refiner." But the Book of Job, raising more questions than it answers, could not reconcile her
to the death, long ago, of young Annie Steen, "so
useful, so indispensable, whom everybody loved," nor
to the loss, so recent and so sore, of missionaries like
Meta Fleming and Ida Mitchell, "the very best,
most gifted, and altogether suitable." Only the
Christian solution of things so "awfully mysterious"
could give her light and comfort. "They must surely,"
she said, "be greatly needed somewhere else."

That assurance satisfied her. Give her the Christian faith and hope, and she was not only prepared to
see the good die young, but irresistibly moved
to take their place and carry on their work.
"For Annie Steen," she had wistfully written in
her own girlhood, "don't we rejoice? A short,
happy, useful life, and then what joy! I wish I

could be of use in bringing some to the possession of that wonderful hope that we have. I am of so very little use in that way. And yet I am content to leave even that in my good Master's hands. I am willing to be led, and I think surely He will teach me in time, to be of more use. I say I am willing—well, not always, but I do want to be willing." Thus in every age Christ obtains His "willing people," the succession never failing. One golden bough is no sooner severed from the stem than another is found in its place.

Another grace which will never be forgotten by Mary's friends was her possession of a tranquil spirit. One who served her at Agharainy for a dozen years said to a missionary guest, "I have never seen a frown on her face or heard a cross or hasty word spoken by her." And the guest thinks that "this testimony speaks even more for the lady of the house than being editor of *Woman's Work* for over a quarter of a century." Few words were oftener on Mary's lips than "In nothing be anxious . . . and the peace of God . . . shall keep your hearts and minds." One of the quaintest and most characteristic things in all her letters is expressed thus : "And now when one misses a train or a tram, it is good to think that instead of chafing at the waste of ten minutes, it is an opportunity for the Practice of the Presence of God—also for deep breathing ! " Here is indeed a sister of Brother Laurence ! And in the great trials she was just as calm. When deep, dark sorrow came, and the light was dimmed in her happy home, her faith kept her serene and strong. Whittier's lines exactly express the spirit of her life :

Drop Thy still dews of quietness
    Till all our strivings cease;
Take from our souls the strain and stress,
And let our ordered lives confess
    The beauty of Thy peace.

She was withal sensitively careful never to let nature be credited with bestowing on her that peace which is a fruit of the Spirit. In the first year of the War she was requested by her friend Mrs. Walker to give an address on the conditions for obtaining the peace of God, and she answered in a self-revealing letter. After quoting in full that favourite sentence, " Be anxious for nothing," etc., she said : " It is my chief text because I have lived on it since I was fifteen. Some people think I am naturally calm and placid; that is a great mistake. Fightings without and fears within seemed a proper description of my life—fantastic fears often, but none the less distressing. I was driven and shut up to the only remedy, but what a complete and adequate one ! ' He is our Peace.' ' We are complete in Him.' "

Her friends love to live over again, in imagination, happy days or hours in her company. When she is named to them, one notices how some of them seem first to hear her voice, others to see her face. " Her speaking voice," says Mrs. Irwin, of Windsor, " as used in ordinary conversation, was the most clear, silvery, bell-like I have ever heard. It had a wonderful *timbre,* and there were far away notes in it which corresponded with a look I often noticed in her face, as if she were seeing other things while talking with me." "I can see her in a quiet talk," says an artist friend, "sitting in her upright posture and looking intently at me, or, as I sometimes felt, through and beyond me, with her lips characteristically parted for an instant while she *thinks* before answering a question or offering an opinion." Helen Waddell, who knew her well in the last years, is one of those who remember her best by "the light of her eyes," which so perfectly reflected the inner light of a radiant soul. "Brilliance was hardly the word for them. They glowed like a lamp. And what always revealed itself in her eyes, sometimes transfigured her whole self, when she was playing, for instance, and the spirit surprised her into passionate expression—'passion that broke through language and escaped.'"

Few will need to ask in the end if her life was happy. She certainly did not live for happiness. Her great word was not pleasure but duty—duty transfigured by love. If duty called her to suffer, she knew how to sacrifice happiness and find blessedness. The promises of the beatitudes were realised by her. Christ's joy was in her and her joy full. That was, in the French metaphor, one side of the medal. The other side was the fellowship of Christ's sufferings. Everyone who lives very near Him and shares His joy becomes also a partaker of His afflictions. In the old legend, the angel who fell in love with Cecilia for her music, and nightly brought her roses from Paradise, gave her at the last the martyr's crown. How the crown of sorrow is transmuted into the unfading crown of glory doth not yet appear, but we know in part.

Such a life, as a gift of the Risen Christ to His Church, is invaluable to all whom it touches, because it makes real so many of the great words of Scripture, especially these: "Love is very patient, very kind. Love knows no jealousy; love makes no parade, gives itself no airs, is never rude, never selfish, never irritated, never resentful; love is never glad when others go wrong, love is gladdened by goodness, always slow to expose, always eager to believe the best, always hopeful, always patient. . . . Thus faith and hope and love last on, these three, but the greatest of all is love."*

Dr. George Thompson, Convener of Foreign Missions, expresses his Church's gratitude for such a gift in these words: "Through many strenuous and often anxious years Mrs. Brown was the fellow-worker of our missionaries, counting no task too hard and no sacrifice too great for the cause of Missions; only she would not speak of sacrifice, her word would be pleasure or privilege.

"Our Church has had an unbroken succession of 'elect women' who have grasped the thought that the way to the conversion of India and China is to win the wives and mothers and children of those lands. This thought Mrs. Brown grasped in all its fulness. And I have heard her appeal with the eloquence of tears to her Christian sisters at home to follow the lead and opening which had been given.

"One often wondered how she could accomplish so

* I Cor. xiii. 4-7, 13. Dr. Moffatt's translation.

much, knowing that her home duties must have taken up a great deal of her time and thought. Most of all was I struck, on meeting her after her two sons were called away, to see how quickly she returned to duty again. Expressions of sympathy were by no means rejected, but those wounds which were too deep for human healing were never allowed to interfere with the doing of what had to be done. ' This one thing I do ' might have been her motto all her days.

"Her fellow-workers all felt that, for her, business concerning the Kingdom was being transacted after prayer and communion with God. And to them she revealed not alone intimate knowledge of the manifold problems of the Mission Field, but a great warmth and tenderness of heart, and a spiritual fervour not the less intense because it burned steadily and rarely flashed into flame. She had a vision as clear and a purpose as resolute as inspired Carey."

She was the St. Brigid of the twentieth century. True to the highest and holiest traditions, she incarnated the real spirit of Ireland, the spirit that triumphed in the past and will triumph again in the future. Let some words taken from the end of one of her last letters, expressing the ardent hope and single desire of a life-long torch-bearer, be as a wireless message to the Churches from the land where her eager spirit still serves the same Master. " IT IS ONLY BY ALL THOSE WHO LOVE JESUS WORKING TOGETHER IN HIS STRENGTH THAT HIS KINGDOM WILL COME IN ALL THE EARTH."

FINIS